The Birobidzhan Affair

The life you face shall be precarious;
you shall be in terror, night and day,
with no assurance of survival.

Deuteronomy 28:66

THE BIROBIDZHAN

A YIDDISH WRITER IN

Translated from the Yiddish by MAX ROSENFELD

Introduction by MICHAEL STANISLAWSKI

5741 / 1981 *Philadelphia*
The Jewish Publication Society of America

ISRAEL EMIOT

AFFAIR

SIBERIA

Library of Congress Cataloging in Publication Data
Emiot, Israel.
     The Birobidzhan affair.
     Translation of: Der Birobidzshaner inyen.
     1. Political prisoners—Russian S.F.S.R.—Biography. 2. Emiot, Israel
—Biography—Imprisonment. 3. Authors, Yiddish—Biography. 4. Jews—
Russian S.F.S.R.—Birobidzhan. 5. Birobidzhan (R.S.F.S.R.)—Ethnic rela-
tions. I. Title.
HV8964.R83E5413   365'.45'0924 [B]   81-2511
ISBN 0-8276-0191-3   AACR2

Designed by Adrianne Onderdonk Dudden

Author's preface

This is the tragic finale to a dream that periodically had fostered hope in the hearts and minds of many. This is the story of Birobidzhan, an issue that finally called for the imposition of severe punishment of those implicated in the shattered vision of national revival.

Nearly all the chapters of this book were serialized in Yiddish in the New York *Jewish Daily Forward* from February 7 through April 15, 1959. After necessary revision, I now present them to the reader.

This is written during a period in world history when superhuman efforts are being made for a world of peace and democracy, for a world in which none of the atrocities of the Hitler era, which had brought about the annihilation of one-third of the Jewish people and many million of our fellowmen, never again could be repeated. This book aims to warn the world against that government and its system, which led to the horrible events herein depicted. Should my story, even in small measure, serve as a reminder to the world, I shall feel that my mission has been accomplished.

This is a chronicle of heart-rending events. There was no attempt here at polishing, artistry, or literary embellishment. Very often, while setting down this gruesome record, the recollections of my frightful experiences accelerated my heartbeat and raced ahead of my pen.

If at times the current of my narrative seems too rapid, I hope the reader will understand and forgive.

Rochester, New York
January 1960

Introduction

Michael Stanislawski

Israel Emiot's prison memoir, *The Birobidzhan Affair*, is a poignant, captivating chronicle of the persecution of Jews and Jewish culture in the last years of Stalin's Russia. It stands out among the dozens of such accounts for the simple reason that its author was a sensitive, talented writer who managed to convey his gruesome experiences in a controlled yet forceful manner, a style at once laconic and impassioned. The result is a gripping story of one man's tortures and hopes and a valuable historical document, both in its own right and for the mass of important data it contains. In this respect, Emiot's work resembles Solzhenitsyn's monumental *Gulag Archipelago*, albeit in a far more limited and modest frame. But this work is not merely Solzhenitsyn *à la juive*: the specific Jewish content—and drama—of this book is its chronicling of the inner devastation wreaked by Stalinism on Jews within and beyond the borders of the Soviet Union. The true, if unstated, subject of this memoir is the tragedy of modern Jews' nearly boundless capacity for self-delusion.

Unfortunately, though perhaps inevitably, Emiot did not dwell at length on either the ideological or the emotional context of his travails—the first leg, as it were, of his journey to and from Birobidzhan. To appreciate the tale the reader must be armed with considerable background information, knowledge of events and episodes once much heralded but now, indeed, relegated to the trashbin of history. The purpose of this introductory essay, therefore, is to attempt to weave together three parallel stories: the political history of Birobidzhan, the Jewish Autonomous Region of the USSR; the biography of the Polish Jew Israel Yanovsky-Goldwasser; and the literary creation of the Yiddish poet Israel Emiot.

Israel Emiot was the pseudonym of Israel Yanovsky-Goldwasser, who was born in the town of Ostrów Mazowiecka, near Warsaw, on January 15, 1909, and died in Rochester, New York, on March 7, 1978.[1] The name "Emiot" is a composite of the Polish initials of Israel's father, Melekh Yanovsky; Goldwasser was his mother's maiden name.

The Yanovsky and Goldwasser families were related to some of the leading lights of Polish Hasidism. Melekh Yanovsky was renowned in Ostrów as a Talmud scholar, but soon after his marriage abandoned the world of tradition for that of enlightenment. In 1919 he left Poland for America, leaving his family behind. Although he intended to become a physician, he fell on hard times, became a presser, and died at an early age. His wife and son remained in Ostrów, in the insulated world of Jewish tradition.

Israel's mother was a pious woman who had overlooked her husband's heresies for the sake of love. After his death, she struggled to raise her son to be a good, learned Jew. Israel studied in a heder and then in a yeshiva until his midteens. Soon he showed signs of precosity, perhaps even of idiosyncracy. As a boy he wrote poetry in Hebrew but then turned to Yiddish. In 1926 he published his first verses (under the name I. Yanovsky) in I. M. Weissenberg's anthology *Our Hope*. These were lyrical religious poems, expressing the sensitive Hasidism of the young Israel. After this debut, he became a frequent contributor to the substantial Orthodox press in Poland and a well-known religious poet.

1. For biographical and bibliographical information, see the entry for Israel Emiot in *Leksikon fun der yidisher literatur*, ed. Z. Reysin, vol. 6 (New York, 1965), pp. 601–6.

In private, however, Israel had begun to read the "many curious books" his father had left behind, and in the early 1930s he followed his father's footsteps into the secular world. Encouraged by I. J. Singer and Peretz Markish, Emiot began to contribute poems, essays, and short stories to the foremost Yiddish journals and newspapers in Poland and America, publishing four volumes of verse between 1932 and 1938. His poetry at this stage was largely a lyrical elegy to the world he loved but had to abandon. A typical poem, written in 1936, read (in literal translation):

> My grandmother!
> In your prayerbook, day is met in the fields
> Above, a prayer—
> Below, its translation.
> Can anything be so simple, so understandable
> As a summer day
> In beds of wheat?
> But still, my sad soul
> Always believed that God was too deep
> To be found in the prayerbook's translation.
> The fields stammer out the meaning of the day
> But the point still eludes me.[2]

In September 1939, Emiot was in Warsaw. After the Nazis invaded, he hurried home to Ostrów and tried to convince his mother to escape to the nearby Soviet-occupied territory. She refused to do so, as he later recalled, because she had borrowed some money from a servant girl and would not leave town before repaying her debt.[3] Israel fled to Bialystok, in the Soviet-occupied part of Poland. Soon, he learned that his mother—and the servant girl—were among the six hundred Jews shot by the Germans in Ostrów that autumn.

In Bialystok, Emiot joined the ranks of the Soviet Yid-

2. "Poem XI," in Emiot, *Bay der velt-lider* (Krakow-Lodz, 1936).
3. See the story "My Mother," in Emiot, *Life in a Mirror* (Rochester, N.Y., 1976), p. 49.

dish writers congregated there, including his old friend Peretz Markish, who had left Poland for the Soviet Union in 1926 and in 1939 was awarded the Order of Lenin. It seems that Emiot came increasingly closer to the political views of Markish and his friends. Despite the Ribbentrop-Molotov Pact and the well-known purges of Yiddish writers in the preceding years, the Soviet Union still was seen by a large number of Yiddish writers as the only hope for freedom and the last hope for Yiddish. In 1940, when Soviet newspapers continued to publish photographs of Molotov standing next to Hitler and reports of Soviet grain and oil shipments to Germany, a volume of Emiot's poems was published in Moscow by the government press *Der Emes* (The Truth). "Meeting My First Red Army Officer" was a typical poem in this collection. Here, Emiot wrote:

> The world, newly created, stands before you,
> Thirty years of life till now—untrue;
> Your spirit is sewn with strings,
> Each one taut, waiting for a bow.[4]

These verses permitted the editor of the volume to declare:

> On the other side of the Soviet border, in formerly feudal Poland where Emiot was born and raised . . . his poetry sang with only half a voice, in a quiet, solemn tone, instead of "singing out loud, as one should," as he writes now, singing the praises of the "great and growing accomplishments he sees in this land." The poems in which he writes of his encounters with the new Soviet man prove that the new Soviet concepts are beginning to take root in his poetic consciousness. . . . In these verses, Emiot strides forth into a new poetic mode, that of an important Soviet poet.[5]

In the summer of 1941, after the German invasion of Russia, Emiot was evacuated to Alma-Ata, Kazakhstan, where

4. Emiot, *Lider* (Moscow, 1940).
5. Ibid., pp. 3–4.

he lived in great poverty and continued to write. His reports on the Jewish refugees in the Soviet Far East were published in the Moscow Yiddish press and transmitted abroad by the Jewish Anti-Fascist Committee. In February 1944, along with other Yiddish writers, he was called to Moscow by the Anti-Fascist Committee to protest the Nazi persecutions of the Jews. This is where *The Birobidzhan Affair* begins: we learn that at this meeting in Moscow Emiot roomed with representatives of the Jewish Autonomous Region in Birobidzhan, who appealed for renewed support for their dormant venture. Emiot now became a supporter of the Birobidzhan project and accepted the position of Birobidzhan correspondent for the Anti-Fascist Committee. He left Moscow for the Far East and arrived in Birobidzhan in July 1944.

In his memoirs Emiot explains his decision in one short paragraph:

> The Birobidzhan representatives, with whom I shared a room in the Hotel Moscow, tried to persuade me to return with them and help in the work of restoring Yiddish culture there. They particularly urged me to read the speech that Kalinin had delivered in 1926 at a conference of *Gezerd.* . . . I did so and was moved by its sympathy for the Jewish plight. Kalinin stated that Birobidzhan must become a Jewish republic where Jews, living on the land in large numbers, could evolve their own governing bodies and safeguard their own national culture. I was captivated by the idea, despite Ilya Ehrenburg's stormy outburst at the meeting: "You people are trying to create a new ghetto!"

To understand Emiot's move, we must backtrack a bit and review the history of that obscure corner of the Jewish world that is Birobidzhan, the Jewish Autonomous Region of the Soviet Union.

Birobidzhan is an area in the southern part of the Soviet Far East bordered by the river Amur, which for 550 kilometers constitutes the border between the Soviet Union and

Manchuria. With an area of 34,000 square kilometers, Birobidzhan is roughly the size of Holland and Belgium combined, or in Jewish terms, one-third larger than Palestine after the amputation of Transjordan and three times larger than the area offered to the Jews in the Uganda proposal. The climate is continental, with cold, dry winters and hot, rainy summers. Rich in natural resources, Birobidzhan contains coal, iron, tin, copper, asbestos, and gold. In 1926, 53 percent of the area was covered with thick virgin forests, 16 percent with swamps, and 14 percent with meadowland. The population consisted of Russians, Trans-Baikal Cossacks, Koreans, Byelorussians, Chinese, and native tribes such as the Tungi and Goldi.[6]

The idea of colonizing this territory with Jews first arose in the 1920s, when the Soviet leadership and its Jewish agents were seeking some solution to the grave new economic problems of the Jewish population of the USSR. During the first years of Bolshevik rule, various attempts were made to settle Jews on the land in the areas in which they already lived. Thus, by 1923 there were 76,000 Jews living as farmers in the Soviet Union. But the problem of déclassé Jews was reaching such heights that it became clear a new solution would have to be found. In 1924 the government created various committees and organizations to help settle Jews as agriculturalists. The original plan was to settle a half million Jews in the Ukraine and the Crimea, but for various reasons—the most important being the vociferous opposition of the Crimean Tartars and the Ukrainians—other areas were sought for Jewish mass settlement. In 1927 a commission was sent to explore other regions, including the Azov area and the steppes of Kazakhstan. Finally, the region of Birobidzhan was chosen as the most appropriate site for Jewish settlement.[7]

6. A Kirzhnits, "Vegn der yidisher avtonomer gegnt," in *Yidn in FSSR*, ed. S. Dimanshtein (Moscow, 1935), pp. 63–72.
7. Chimen Abramsky, "The Birobidzhan Project, 1927–1959," in *The Jews in the Soviet Union Since 1917*, ed. L. Kochan (Oxford, 1970), p. 66.

On March 28, 1928, the Central Executive Committee of the Supreme Soviet of the USSR officially declared that Birobidzhan be set aside for Jewish colonization, with the intent of "creating on this territory a Jewish national administrative-territorial unit." The proclamation was followed by a barrage of publicity encouraging Jews to take advantage of this opportunity. Official reports claimed that the first Jewish settlers arrived in Birobidzhan on the very day of the announcement.

Despite this official pronouncement, there were still many people who continued to support the Crimean project. Debate continued until 1931, when the presidium of the Central Committee of the Communist Party of the Soviet Union called for preparations for transforming Birobidzhan into the Jewish Autonomous Region of the USSR. Three years later, the president of the Soviet Union formally declared Birobidzhan the Jewish Autonomous Region.

There is much confusion in the literature regarding the precise number of Jewish immigrants to Birobidzhan. No definitive official statistics exist, and experts' estimates vary greatly. The most reliable study of the question claims that between 1928 and 1938, 43,200 Jews moved to Birobidzhan and 19,000 stayed there; this figure was disappointing to officials who hoped for truly massive immigration.[8] Clearly, despite the significance which the Soviet authorities gave to the project, it failed to inspire the Jewish masses of the USSR.

The project did receive enthusiastic support—from Jewish Communists and Yiddishists outside Russia, and even from some Zionists who greeted the establishment of Birobidzhan as a positive, healthy step toward the improvement of the sorry state of Soviet Jews. Committees enlisting active aid for Birobidzhan were set up around the world; the most impor-

8. Ya'akov Levavi, *Ha-hityashvut ha-yehudit be-Birobidzhan* (Jerusalem, 1965), p. 107. This is by far the most successful study of the entire question. Abramsky, cited above, is the best review in English of the history of the project.

tant were in the United States, Argentina, and Palestine. Apart from money raising and propagandizing, foreign Jews contributed manpower as well to the Jewish Autonomous Region: approximately twelve hundred Jews (mostly from Lithuania, South America, and the United States) migrated to Birobidzhan until 1932, when foreign immigration was curtailed; seventy-four Jews actually moved to Birobidzhan from Palestine at this time.[9]

Clearly, though, the fate of the Jewish Autonomous Region depended almost entirely on its support in official circles in Russia. The motives of the Soviet leaders in this regard are not very clear; indeed, it well may be they had no clear-cut, consistent policy toward the Jews and engaged in often self-contradictory attempts at finding the most effective means of dealing with them. Only one top official ever expressed himself publicly on the subject, the figurehead president of the USSR, Mikhail Kalinin, the government's representative of and to the plain people who made up the majority of the citizens of the Soviet Union. Kalinin was a true philo-Semite, believing in Birobidzhan as the best means of Jewish national preservation. In the speech Israel Emiot read fourteen years after its delivery in 1926, Kalinin said:

> The Jewish people now faces the great task of maintaining its nationality, and this requires the transformation of a considerable part of the Jewish population into a completely settled agricultural peasantry numbering in the hundreds of thousands at least. Only thus can the Jewish masses hope for the survival of their nationality.[10]

Obviously, Stalin and the other true leaders of the country were far from such sentiments; indeed, orthodox Soviet ideology denied the nationality of the Jews. Birobidzhan was supported for a combination of reasons: Far Eastern foreign

9. S. Blumberg, "Di yidishe arbetndike in oysland helfn boyen di yidishe avtonome gegnt," in *Yidn in FSSR*, p. 279; Levavi, *Ha-bityashvut*, p. 115.
10. Abramsky, "The Birobidzhan Project," p. 67.

policy, the hope of winning support among Western Jewry, and the need to ameliorate the economic crisis of the Jews in the Soviet Union. Whatever the exact constellation of motivations, it is beyond doubt that the main initiative for the Birobidzhan project came not from Jews but from the leaders of the various commisariats responsible for the defense and security of the Soviet Union, as well as its agricultural development.

In the mid-1930s, Birobidzhan was hailed as a growing center of Yiddish culture. Jewish artists were encouraged to settle there, plans were announced for a great library, a school system, theater, even a Yiddish opera. These hopes were buoyed by the statements of President Kalinin himself, who predicted that in due course Birobidzhan would become a full-fledged Soviet republic.

All these hopes, both cultural and political, were dashed in late 1936. The death sentence came from Stalin himself: in his famous speech "On the Draft Constitution of the USSR," delivered on November 25, Stalin ruled that for any autonomous region to become a republic it must have a population of more than one million. Not even the most optimistic believer could hope that Birobidzhan one day would be a Jewish state.

At the same time, Stalin's purges began to take their toll on the Jewish Autonomous Region. In August 1936, Yoysef Liberberg, chairman of the Birobidzhan Soviet, was arrested, accused of being a "nationalist Trotskyite and a former member of the Po'alei Zion." By mid-1937, the purges were in full swing. The entire Far East was declared out of bounds for security reasons, and immigration to Birobidzhan was placed under the control of the NKVD. The next year, the committees and organizations supporting Birobidzhan were abolished, and nearly all their leaders, as well as the local officials in Birobidzhan, were liquidated.[11] All these arrests and murders were,

11. Levavi, *Ha-hityashvut*, p. 64.

as Emiot testified, "common knowledge"; nevertheless, the Jewish Autonomous Region continued to survive, and Jewish Communists, fellow travelers, and Yiddishists continued to hold out hope that it would bring salvation to the Jews and Yiddish culture.

After World War II and the interest of the Jewish Anti-Fascist Committee in Birobidzhan described by Emiot, Jewish immigration to the Jewish Autonomous Region picked up once more. Between 1945 and 1948, approximately 10,000 Jews arrived in Birobidzhan, bringing the total Jewish population to about 30,000.[12] Along with this demographic growth was a flurry of cultural advance: the Yiddish press, theater, and literature were revived in Birobidzhan and hopes once more ran high for Yiddish life within the framework of Soviet Socialism.

Once more, however, reality intervened: a new series of purges took place, now aimed exclusively at the Jews and Jewish cultural and national activity. As Emiot describes, Jewish writers and politicians were arrested one by one, until almost none was free. The sentences were harsh, the penalties always enforced. The saga of Birobidzhan came to a tragic end. This time almost no one continued to believe—only a diminishing group of diehards outside of Russia. In Birobidzhan the remaining Jewish population was tiny and growing smaller by the year. Jewish cultural activity was non-existent, except for the charade of the Yiddish translation of the local version of *Pravda*. In April 1958, Khrushchev explained to a correspondent of *Le Figaro* that the Birobidzhan experiment failed because the Jews were too individualistic and incapable of collective work. Since that time, the Soviet press periodically has referred to the possibility of a revival of the Jewish Autonomous Region in Birobidzhan. Indeed, the name still appears on maps, in censuses, and in Soviet geography textbooks. But today no one believes.

12. Ibid., p. 107.

Israel Emiot was liberated from prison camp on March 27, 1953. As he describes in the last pages of his memoirs, he returned to Birobidzhan, but since he was not rehabilitated, life was tortuous. In 1956 he was repatriated to Poland, where he published a new volume of poetry. Two years later he joined his wife and two children (from whom he had been separated in 1940) in America, and settled in Rochester, New York. In that same year he made a highly successful trip to Israel. Besides this memoir he wrote several volumes of verse in the United States. *Life in a Mirror*, an anthology of English translations of his poems and short stories, was published in Rochester in 1976. He died in 1978, still not having reached his full poetic potential; the wounds, we may surmise, never healed completely. One of his American poems contains a fitting epitaph:

> Snuff me out, You must, O my Lord,
> But not before the day reveals its mystery.
> Until my last moment
> Let me thirst for all that is wondrous,
> For all there is yet to know.
> First the noise—
> Then, the silence—the world's macabre
> Cat and mouse game.[13]

13. Emiot, *Life in a Mirror*, p. 23.

The Birobidzhan Affair

I go to Birobidzhan

In February 1944 I was invited, along with several other Yiddish writers, to come to Moscow for a meeting of the Jewish Anti-Fascist Committee, which was protesting Hitler's atrocities against the Jews. I was then living in Alma-Ata, capital of Kazakhstan, with a group of Jewish writers who had been evacuated to the Far Eastern regions of the Soviet Union in face of the Nazi onslaught. All of us suffered privation during the war years, but we never stopped writing. In addition to poetry I was writing newspaper articles about the life of the evacuated Jews in Kazakhstan. These articles were sent by the Jewish Anti-Fascist Committee to publications abroad.

Evidently my work caught someone's eye, because as soon as I arrived in Moscow I was asked to become a regular correspondent for the Jewish Autonomous Region of Birobidzhan. On the agenda at the meeting of the committee was the matter of designating Crimea as another Jewish autonomous region. At one time this idea had been supported vigorously by Yuri Larin, the noted Soviet economist. Stalin, however, was opposed to the plan, ostensibly out of fear that in time of war the Jews there would not be a "sufficiently loyal element." Many years later Nikita Khrushchev admitted publicly that he had concurred with Stalin on this.

In any case, the Crimea idea came to nothing. Interestingly, though, at the Jewish Anti-Fascist Committee meeting it was the representatives of the Jewish Autonomous Region who argued that, despite all its past failures and difficulties, this was a propitious time to develop Birobidzhan. They sent a delegation to President Kalinin, who assured them he was holding to his position. Kalinin long had advocated the establishment of a Jewish autonomous region, in which he saw not only the basis for economic development but a place where the character of the Jewish nationality in the Soviet Union could be preserved and advanced.

The Birobidzhan representatives, with whom I shared a room in the Hotel Moscow, tried to persuade me to return with them and help in the work of restoring Yiddish culture there. They particularly urged me to read the speech that Kalinin had delivered in 1926 at a conference of *Gezerd*, the agency for "settlement of Jewish toilers on the land." I did so and was moved by its sympathy for the Jewish plight. Kalinin stated that Birobidzhan must become a Jewish republic where Jews, living on the land in large numbers, could evolve their own governing bodies and safeguard their own national culture. I was captivated by the idea, despite Ilya Ehrenburg's stormy outburst at the meeting: "You people are trying to create a new ghetto!"

Leib Kvitko, Aaron Kushnirov, David Bergelson, and other Yiddish writers I met in Moscow welcomed my decision to go to Birobidzhan and wished me well. Bergelson had lived there himself for over a year and written several novellas there. He was familiar with the geography of the area and expressed enthusiasm for its natural beauty and its wealth of resources. "A Jewish writer, especially a poet," he assured me, "will find much there to inspire him."

After I was settled in Birobidzhan, the Yiddish poet Peretz Markish sent me frequent letters of encouragement, adding that if it weren't for his strong ties with the city of Moscow he too would settle in Birobidzhan. While I was trying to make up my mind, however, he wasn't so enamored of the idea. "It's so far away from everything!" he remonstrated.

Nonetheless, in his customary selfless and helpful manner Markish somehow obtained enough money for me from a writers' fund to pay my expenses for the trip. Then Solomon Lozovsky, deputy chief of the Soviet Information Bureau, who had jurisdiction over all the anti-Fascist committees in the Soviet Union, refused permission for me to go as a correspondent to Birobidzhan because I was not a Communist Party member and because I had come from Poland so recently. The Jewish Anti-Fascist Committee therefore could not subsidize me officially.

Again, Markish came to my aid. Through the intervention of his friend, the novelist Alexander Fadeyev, he eventually obtained the necessary approval. With a note from Markish in my hand, I was received by Fadeyev, who asked me affably, "You know Markish?"

A bit puzzled by his question, I replied, "Of course I know Markish. This note is from him."

"I mean, do you know Markish's work, do you know any of his poems?"

To my great embarrassment, I could not recall any of Markish's poems from memory.

Fadeyev smiled. "I do. I know many of his poems by heart!" And he proceeded to recite a long fragment from one of Peretz Markish's works.

When I arrived at the city of Birobidzhan in July 1944, the Jewish cultural situation was lamentable, to say the least. The Birobidzhan *Star*, the only Yiddish newspaper there, had been shut down by decree during the war. Only one Russian daily—with an occasional Yiddish page—was being published. The whole thing was most painful. The Yiddish typecases in the print shop were full, expert Yiddish typesetters were walking around idle, and no Yiddish publications were being printed.

The Yiddish theater, however, was still active, performing Goldfaden's *Witch*, Gutzkow's *Uriel Acosta*, and several other classical Yiddish, Russian, and foreign plays. Jews still secretly recalled with delight Moshe Kulbak's *Boitra the Bandit,* which the theater had presented fifty times before large audiences until Kulbak was arrested.

Still functioning was a Yiddish middle school, where Jewish youngsters could be heard fervently reciting the words of Mendele, Peretz, Sholom Aleichem, Bergelson, Hofstein, and other writers. But the official language of the region was no longer Yiddish, as it had been in 1936, when the courts, the police department, the city administration, and various other official activities were conducted in that language. The Pedagogical Institute, which until 1937 had a department for training Yiddish elementary grade teachers, was closed.

Nevertheless, there were definite signs of a revival. Early in 1945 a Yiddish anthology was published. The Yiddish theater showed evidence of new life. Several local Yiddish playwrights were writing for the theater's repertoire. Alex Stein, the creative director of the Vilna Troupe, was brought in. Several new actors were engaged. Leaders of the region even prevailed upon General Nikishov, administrator of the notorious Kolyma prison camp in Siberia, to release a talented Jewish actor who had been imprisoned in 1938 during the Yezhov era. More Yiddish writers, painters, and scholars had come to settle. There was talk of opening a Yiddish college. The Jewish population was still comparatively small, however. Of a total population of about one hundred thousand, there were no more than twenty-five thousand Jews in Birobidzhan at the end of World War II.

The short-lived revival

Of the Jews who were evacuated from the Ukraine, Byelorussia, or Poland, very few went to Birobidzhan. The events of 1937–38—when most of the Jewish immigrants from abroad, as well as many of the original settlers in Birobidzhan, were arrested and later "liquidated"—were common knowledge.

Despite all this, a Jew still could feel at home in Birobidzhan. It was no secret that wherever the Germans had occupied an area of the Soviet Union the anti-Semites were given a new lease on life. Jew-haters (especially in the Ukraine) who until the war had concealed their true feelings now found their tongues again. In Birobidzhan this did not happen. I recall an incident where one such character got drunk and in broad daylight began bellowing, "*Bey zhidov!* Beat the kikes!" In no time he was surrounded by a crowd of Jewish war invalids who took off his coat and whacked him so unmercifully that he had a miraculous change of heart. "*Lyublyu yevreyev!* I love the Jews!" he protested. The Jews of Birobidzhan did not hesitate to use their fists in answer to anti-Semitic slurs.

As a newspaper correspondent I read all the telegrams that came to the office of the local administrative committee concerning immigration. These telegrams were signed by Stalin or Malenkov, who was then Stalin's right-hand man. In January 1946 a decree was issued encouraging voluntary immigration of Jews from the Ukraine to Birobidzhan, with the project to be underwritten by the government. Rail transportation was free. Each immigrant was to receive a bonus of 330 rubles. In addition, a family could obtain a ten-year loan of 10,000 rubles for the purchase of farm equipment and supplies if they agreed to settle on the land.

Ten thousand Jewish families from the Ukraine responded to the call. The human resources of this migration were quite diversified: expert handicraftsmen, industrial technicians, engineers, physicians, teachers, experienced farmers, highly placed administrators. Some of the latter had to go to a great deal of trouble to be released from their employment. One, for example, gave up the directorship of the main granary in the Ukraine to take a more modest position as manager of a farming district in Birobidzhan. Other Jewish specialists in their fields made similar choices.

Old settlers in Birobidzhan told me they hadn't seen so much activity, with so much Yiddish spoken freely in the streets, since 1936. The question even arose of opening a series of Yiddish elementary schools throughout the region to serve the large number of recent Jewish immigrants.

Every region in the USSR has its own annual economic plan, which is then included in the plans for its respective republic and the entire country. Aside from the general government subsidies for construction, the Birobidzhan region received massive assistance from Jews in the United States, including not only food and clothing but also factory equipment, power plants, diesel motors, mechanical saws of all sorts, and prefabricated houses. From one such group of homes, bought in Holland by American Jews, a whole street was constructed in the Jewish Autonomous Region. Long after Lend-Lease had ended, American Jews continued to send gifts to Birobidzhan (as they did also for Stalingrad, which had been destroyed almost totally during the war).

The city of Birobidzhan together with its suburbs at that time had over forty thousand inhabitants. Anyone who knows the run-down condition of Soviet Far Eastern towns will agree that Birobidzhan, with its symmetrical design, its brilliant foliage, and its newly paved streets, was one of the most beautiful cities in that part of the country. The Birobidzhan regional hospital had a well-deserved reputation. Its staff of physicians, most of them Jews, included several noted specialists, such as its chief, Dr. Mitzenhendler, and Dr. Rabinowich, a well-known surgeon. The hospital contained several hundred beds plus a large maternity clinic, which was added later. In addition to a dozen or so artels (collective farms), the city also had several industrial plants for the manufacture of textiles, knit goods, clothing, wagons, and food processing.

The Jewish character of all this construction changed drastically in 1948, however. Although economically the development of the area continued according to plan, it was no longer as the Jewish Autonomous Region but as part of the Khabarovsk region.

That year, 1948, the activities of the Jewish cultural institutions were canceled abruptly. The impressive Birobidzhan Yiddish theater became the Home for Pioneers, and its artists fled for their lives across the sprawling Soviet Union. The leaders of the region, among them cultural workers and Yiddish writers, were arrested. All the Jewish activity that had taken place between 1945 and 1948 was declared "nationalistic and counterrevolutionary."

In jail

The heavy iron door closed behind me with a dull thud. Suddenly I recalled a similarly chilling thump that I heard with horror during my early student days in Warsaw. It had happened on Pawia Street, in the courtyard where I lived with my uncle and studied in a yeshiva. Someone had jumped from a fifth-story window. Later I saw the pool of blood, the crowd of people. Most vivid in my memory was the thud of the body hitting the pavement.

For several months before my arrest I walked around every day looking over my shoulder. After all, there must have been a reason why I was dismissed from my position and why it was impossible for me to get another job—any job, even as a laborer. Every night in my sleep my ears picked up the slightest sound. Somebody's out there! They're coming for me!

I roamed the streets of Birobidzhan and envied the woman selling peas in the marketplace. She was lucky; they would never come for her. I wandered around the city and said goodbye to the marvelous park that cuts into the River Biro like a little island. Again and again I stood and admired the charming bridges across the streams, which reminded me so much of the paintings of Polenov, the great Russian artist who loved to depict scenes where the trees are reflected in the river below and the soul of the world slumbers in the deep.

A hundred times I bade farewell to the famous Birobidzhan volcano, the mountain from which one can see the whole city as plainly as the palm of one's hand. More than once I climbed to the peak and marveled at this city that had been built by Jewish hands. By 1947, when I arrived here, the taiga had been pushed back a considerable distance. I was especially proud of the Jewish toilers who had cleared the forest and constructed a city, one of the most attractive in the Far East.

Had that been only a year ago? Transports of new immigrants were arriving almost daily. Jubilant crowds jammed the railroad stations. The city's Young Pioneer groups came to toss fresh flowers at the incoming trains. All the orchestras in the area joined the celebration and played lively Jewish tunes. The eyes of the immigrants brimmed with tears of joy. The new arrivals were put up temporarily in barracks, in private homes. Jews danced in the street. Yiddish writers read their work before gatherings of new immigrants.

One of these transports brought the world-renowned Yiddish writer Der Nister (Pinkhes Kahanovich), who believed that Jewish culture in the Soviet Union could be preserved only if Jews lived in compact masses in their own autonomous region. I remember his distinguished appearance, his serene, flowing gestures, his almost whispered speech, as if he were uttering the words of a prayer or the truths of some ancient zaddik.

Then, all at once, it was as if some secret, sinister hand had smashed the windows of my childhood home on a Friday evening and a cruel wind had blown out my mother's Sabbath candles. A series of greetings came from Moscow, one more dire than the other: Jewish Anti-Fascist Committee—abolished! Emes publishing house—closed! Yiddish theater—closed! *Eynikayt*, the only Yiddish newspaper—shut down! Yiddish writers—arrested!

The Russian newspapers began printing ominous insinuations about Jews. Professors and writers, attacked for cosmopolitanism in the press, now had their Jewish surnames appended to their Russian family names, as if it were a conspiracy engineered by the entire Jewish people.

The satrap Lavrenti Beria had a deputy in Birobidzhan in the person of Colonel Goglidze, chief of the secret police in the Far East. His kingdom stretched from Vladivostok, on the Pacific Ocean, deep inland to the city of Chita, a vast territory the size of Europe. Goglidze, a cruel, tenacious despot, had his departments and punishment cells in every large city in the area. Shortly after the secretary of the Communist Party and the chairman of the Executive Committee suddenly had been called to Moscow, Goglidze visited Birobidzhan.

"Suddenly" because from Birobidzhan to the Khabarovsk airport it is no more than 180 kilometers, or three hours by train. But they were sent to Moscow on a special autocar that runs on railroad tracks and takes forever. When they finally reached Moscow they were lectured by a whole commission, headed by Malenkov. Then they were duly warned, and all the details of their deviations were recorded in their personal files. Immediately upon their return to Birobidzhan, meetings were organized at which the "nationalism" of the Jewish leaders was exposed.

They were accused of all sorts of crimes. *Item:* Birobidzhan accepted foreign assistance in the form of shoes and clothing sent by American Jews to their brothers and sisters in the Jewish Autonomous Region. *Item:* There was too much talk in the region about strengthening Jewish culture. *Item:* There were plans to establish a Jewish university. *Item:* The Yiddish newspaper was about to be expanded. *Item:* A Jewish publishing house had been opened. *Item:* The regional museum featured special exhibits on Jewish history.

Why was all this a crime? Because it was artificial. You are trying to implant Jewish culture artificially in a region where the majority of the population is not Jewish!

All these charges appeared in the newspapers. Later, from our own indictments we learned about the diabolical provocation that Beria and his agents had invented as a gift for

Stalin. In his mania for seeing treason and espionage everywhere, Stalin rewarded those who brought him evidence of the most complicated and fantastic plots concocted by this or that section of the population. Scoundrels like Beria, Goglidze, Ryumin, and Abakumov—inhuman sadists, sexual perverts who kidnapped university students for their personal harems —fabricated the wildest provocations for the Little Father in the Kremlin. One of those plots was known as "The Conspiracy of International Jewry against the Union of Socialist Soviet Republics." It was simply a new version of the *Protocols of the Elders of Zion*. The Jewish people (it alleged) have a secret organization aimed at subverting the Revolution. And Birobidzhan was a link in the chain of this worldwide conspiracy. Birobidzhan had become a veritable nest of spies. Birobidzhan was to be transformed into a fortress of international reaction. Birobidzhan was to be severed from the Soviet Union and handed over to the United States! To this end, visitors from America had contacted the Jewish Anti-Fascist Committee after the war and brought with them the completed plans that Solomon Mikhoels and Itzik Fefer had given them in 1943, after those Jewish leaders had been recruited by U.S. espionage agencies. No more, no less.

The appearance of Colonel Goglidze at the spontaneous meetings was a signal that this matter was not going to end with the reproaches that Malenkov had delivered to the leaders of the Jewish Autonomous Region when they were in Moscow.

And so here I am in my prison cell, probably only one of many.

They brought me here through mile-long corridors and up mountainous flights of stairs, past a whole series of similar cells. My first cell is number 23, which is on the topmost level at the far side of the building. It holds one person, a cot, and four high walls, in one of which is a little window about the size of two fists. Through this barred window I can see nothing except an inch of sky. In one corner of the cell is the toilet—a bucket with a lid on it.

I am in the investigative jail in Goglidze's kingdom. The only article of clothing they allowed me to bring is a bathrobe with some cigarettes and matches in the pocket. Before they locked me in my cell I was stripped and searched from head to toe, including my mouth, ears, and rectum, to make certain I hadn't smuggled in a needle, a piece of jagged glass, or a cyanide tablet. I said to myself, like Job, "Naked came I out of my mother's womb, and naked shall I return."

First interrogation

So far I'm fine. Things are quiet. I have crossed over into another world. The walls here have turned my soul inward. I crush the recent past between my fingers like a petal and fly back in time to my childhood, my youth . . . I am studying with the Master, Rabbi Meir Dan Plotsky, of blessed memory, world-renowned scholar and Hasidic leader. He is wonderfully kind to me. I bathe in the luminescent holiness of his shining countenance . . . I see my grandfather, Reb Mordecai Leyb, who ate only enough food to keep himself alive, so he could immerse himself in Torah and Hasidic lore from dawn to midnight . . . I am an orphan whose father had just died, a father I virtually did not know. I hear the voice of my grandmother, who raised me and spoke to me in words that were like the fluttering of the Divine Spirit's wings.

But now I hear something else. Through the thick walls of the prison, the sound of tapping, a strange, rhythmic tapping, like the *mene mene tekel ufarsin* that appeared mysteriously on King Belshazzar's palace wall. Not until many months later did I learn the secret of this Morse code communication and become facile enough in it to converse with other prisoners. On this occasion I did not reply. I merely held my breath to see what would happen next.

In a little while the door opened. The guard—blond, husky, wearing the red and blue cap of the MGB, Ministry of State Security, on his head—spoke curtly and without any preliminaries. "Here's a bowl. You eat from it and you drink your tea from it. Sleeping during the day is forbidden. Tapping on the wall is forbidden. You get up at six every morning. Whenever they call you to Interrogation, you go. Breaking furniture is forbidden. Hiding metal objects is forbidden. Once a week you shower. The prisoner is responsible for cleaning his own cell. Once a month the prisoner scours his cot with boiling water. Twenty minutes every day you walk in the yard. For violating any of these rules—the punishment cell!" He recited the whole thing by rote and then slammed the door. A moment later I heard him open another door, where he probably went through the same litany again.

I waited for a summons from the examining magistrate —the interrogator—but night came instead.

Eventually I grew accustomed to being taken out for interrogation. The first time it seemed a most peculiar procedure. It was eleven-thirty at night. I'd been asleep for maybe half an hour. Suddenly the little window in the iron door opened. A voice, almost a whisper, asked if my last name began with E. I said yes. He ordered me: "Put your clothes on!" I put on my clothes. He led me through the long corridor, up the steps, into a special room containing a series of cubicles in which only one person, seated, could fit. He shoved me into this box quickly so I couldn't see who else was being taken for interrogation at the same time.

This special room turned out to be the prison van. On each side of the van were small cubicles with a narrow passageway in between. The prisoners, one at a time, were locked into these windowless, airless boxes. I could hardly breathe. Not infrequently, when the prisoner was large he couldn't even fit into the box. Complaints were voiced: *At least open the door for a moment to let in some air!* But the soldier sitting in the passageway was deaf to these pleas. By the sound of their breathing and their groaning, I slowly learned to recognize my fellow passengers. So it happened sometimes that, despite the strict rules forbidding it, we communicated through the walls of our boxes and learned why the others had been arrested. Later, on the way back from the interrogation, completely exhausted, we heard the muffled moans and sighs of the tormented.

My first time it was all so strange, so unexpected. The van was so high off the ground we had to climb up to get inside. The guards kept shouting and cursing at us: "Move it! Move it! We don't have all goddamn night!" In that fraction of a second I sneaked a look at the prison I was just taken from. It was L-shaped. Across from it was the sprawling, red building for the dangerous criminals, an ancient structure in Khabarovsk. Our prison, by contrast, was new, the last word in construction techniques, built by the Japanese at the beginning of World War II.

They took us to a building six stories high and a block long, built for the administration of the NKVD, the People's Commissariat of Internal Affairs (another name for the secret police). It was a labyrinth of corridors and staircases. Wire netting had been nailed from railing to wall to prevent prisoners from trying to commit suicide by toppling over.

They ushered me into a big, comfortably furnished room. On the floor, an expensive rug. On the desk, all sorts of copper and silver doodads. In one corner, a big wooden flowerpot holding a tall fig tree, whose broad leaves extend halfway across the room. Overhead, a six-armed chandelier made of polished crystal. Had it not been for the portrait of Felix Dzerzhinsky, founder of the Cheka, the original Soviet secret police, I never would have imagined I was sitting in the office of the chief of the Investigation Section, Far East NKVD. Behind the desk sat a man of about sixty in a uniform with the golden epaulets of a colonel. His deeply lined face bespoke a mean disposition, although he was trying to fake a little smile.

"Have a seat!"

When he read me my first indictment, I learned what I already knew from the short note they showed me at the time of my arrest, except that here it was set forth in broader scope and greater detail. (The first indictment is not final; during the investigation additional charges usually are added.) I was being charged under article 58, crimes against the state, section 10, point 1. During the investigation, point 1 was replaced by point 2, which carried a penalty of twenty-five years and, in time of war, death. I was also charged under article 58, section 11, belonging to an illegal organization. When he got to article 58, section 6, espionage, I objected so strenuously that the colonel seemed to pull back a little.

So, according to this indictment, ever since I arrived in the Soviet Union from Poland in 1939 I had been engaged in bourgeois nationalist activity. In the presence of many individuals—whose identity was known to the investigators, of course—I had expressed certain nationalistic views about Jews. I had been particularly active in Birobidzhan from 1944 on. In my writing I had brought out bourgeois nationalist ideas concerning the oneness of the Jewish people, underscored always the Jewish aspect of events, and disseminated insulting fabrications about alleged anti-Semitism in the Ukraine, which supposedly was the reason why Jews there were so eager to emigrate to Birobidzhan. I had written poems about the life of Jewish partisans in the war. I had called for implanting Jewish culture artificially in the Jewish Autonomous Region, at a time when obviously there was no need for it.

When the chief finished, I protested vehemently, denying that any of my activities were counterrevolutionary. I insisted that the concept of bourgeois nationalism was not applicable here because Birobidzhan is an autonomous region and certainly has the right to develop its own national physiognomy. I also pointed out that the whole anti-Jewish campaign recently let loose in the country was a violation of the Soviet constitution itself. I spoke heatedly and with passion, using every argument I could think of.

As the NKVD man heard me out, his mouth twisted into a sarcastic little smile. "So you still maintain that what you did was right? *Podumaitye*—think about it. Go back to your cell and think about it some more. In the meantime, just write your autobiography."

My first inquisitor

At the very first session, the chief of the Investigation Section informed me that he would not be my interrogator, that he would be turning me over to his examining magistrate, because he handled only the big fish and I was definitely not one of those. But the interrogator who came after him was not an underling either; he had risen to the rank of colonel.

Tall, thin, with a sallow complexion, he coughed a lot and seemed to be suffering from asthma. From his manner of speech and his behavior, which were always eminently correct, he did not appear to be cut out for this kind of work. The first time I set eyes on his sickly face I could not help thinking, He must have a wife and small children at home and he holds down a degrading job, but what won't a man do to make a living for his family?

During the week I spent with him I learned more from him than he did from me. The record was copied down exactly as I dictated it. He never tried to slant it in any way. Whenever I didn't like a particular nuance or a word he had written down inaccurately that I thought might be used against me later, he corrected it at once, even if it meant changing a whole sentence or rewriting an entire sheet.

From my first interrogator I learned the names of others who already had been imprisoned. I also discovered that there had existed a trio of Jewish nationalist centers—Moscow, Kiev, and Minsk. What about Birobidzhan? No, no, that was a totally separate affair, and a much more dangerous one, because here an entire territory of the Soviet Union was being jeopardized. Birobidzhan nationalism had been as great a peril before the war as the Ukrainian brand, because in both instances a state government was involved.

My interrogator would begin each morning's work with fifteen minutes of silence, like a ritual. I would sit in a corner on a chair that was anchored to the floor (so it couldn't be used as a weapon by the prisoner). The colonel would sit at his desk, deep in his papers. Precisely at the end of fifteen minutes he would look up at me and begin, "The investigation has revealed that . . . "

The investigation had revealed that I was closely involved with Solomon Mikhoels, that it was he who had recommended me for work in Birobidzhan, that Mikhoels had been employed by a foreign espionage agency, and that the Soviet secret police knew exactly where I had met Mikhoels, where we'd had a drink together, where we went walking together, where we had our conversations, and what instructions I had received from him before I left Moscow to come to Birobidzhan.

The interrogator handed me three photographs. Two were of complete strangers. The third looked familiar.

"Do you know any of these men?"

"I don't recall—"

"Were you ever in Alma-Ata?"

"I was."

"Did you know a Jew from Leningrad by the name of Rayze?"

Before I could reply, he began reading aloud from a document. "In 1942, by order of the People's Commissariat of State Security, I struck up a conversation with Emiot. There is no doubt in my mind that he is a Jewish nationalist. Among the many questions he asked me were these: Did I know that in 1936 all the Yiddish schools in Byelorussia had been liquidated? Did I know that many Zionists had been arrested? I do not know whether Emiot himself ever belonged to a

Zionist organization, but I'm absolutely sure he is a Jewish nationalist."

Very politely, my interrogator then asked me, "What is your response to this information we received from Rayze?"

My reply went something like this. Solomon Mikhoels was a great Soviet patriot who never would have taken orders from a foreign espionage service. Mikhoels was also a good Jew and a superb artist. I considered it an honor to have known him, to have spoken with him. The only instruction he ever gave me was that I should use my talent to write seriously about Jewish life in Birobidzhan. As to what I talked about with this Rayze, how can I be expected to remember that? As the law says, *za davnostyu vremenyi nye pomnyu*—because of the long time that has elapsed since the event, I cannot possibly recall everything I talked about with another person. And even if I did talk with Rayze, what sort of dangerous crime is that? During any normal conversation it is only natural to ask questions, but that is hardly proof that I am a bourgeois nationalist.

The interrogator wrote down exactly what I said. I read it carefully and signed it, and they took me back to my cell. Thus it went every day for a week. Interrogation without a break from morning until noon, and again in the evening until past midnight. That was the routine: two sessions a day and no end to the questions. Each time I appeared in his office there was a new pack of papers on my interrogator's desk. He would begin, "The investigation has revealed . . . "

"The investigation has revealed that you wrote a poem with the phrase, 'the Jewish people of all generations and all lands.' In other words, you proclaim the unity of a *world Jewish people*, which is a bourgeois nationalist fiction.

"The investigation has revealed that you negated the preeminence of Russian literature, that you praised only foreign poetry, that you questioned Mayakovsky's originality, claiming he was an imitator of the American Walt Whitman and the Belgian Émile Verhaeren."

My God! Would there never be an end to it? Would it go on like this forever? When will they begin insulting me, beating me, locking me in a dungeon? The truth was that the enforced sleeplessness was beginning to take its toll already. The twice-a-day interrogations meant that I was getting no more than two or three hours sleep in twenty-four. My nerves were on edge. At the same time, I was ensnared by a foolish delusion: eventually they would have to let me go! There simply was no evidence on which to put me in prison for years. What had I done, anyway?

Worse than anything was the gnawing suspicion that the too-correct behavior of my interrogator was all part of the trap. Does he really believe everything I tell him? True, he admitted to me, "Whether you confess or you don't confess makes little difference. You won't leave here a free man. The investigation already has turned up enough evidence for a trial. If you do confess, however, they may go easier on you at the end. It depends on what level the investigation finally reaches." But the twelve sessions of interrogation produced no concrete evidence at all, not a shred!

Luckily, Sunday was coming, a respite from the incessant questioning. I would shower and sleep—the only day of the week prisoners have these privileges. The loneliness was becoming more and more oppressive. I needed someone, anyone, to talk with. From the neighboring cells they kept tap-tap-tapping to me, but I didn't understand the code yet. I had a foreboding of bad news but shook it off as one does a pesky fly.

My intuition proved correct. Beria's man in the Far East, the all-powerful Goglidze, did not conduct investigations this way. On the second week, a new inquisitor appeared, and life became immeasurably more difficult.

Ozirsky of the NKVD

Much later, when we were already in the prison camp and had behind us the long months of solitary confinement and the indignities, insults, and torments at the hands of that master sadist Ozirsky, the Grand Inquisitor from Khabarovsk, we were even able to make jokes at his expense. This gross, gluttonous creature, who never spoke to me without bellowing, who threw me into the "hole"—the dreaded punishment cell—for five days and nights after each of my defiant answers, this loathsome monster, in addition to being unspeakably vulgar, was also a coward of the worst sort.

During the interrogations his revolver always lay on his desk, in full view and within easy reach. As soon as he detected that he was dealing with someone who might challenge him, he would make certain to have an "assistant"—really a bodyguard—at his desk. Although Ozirsky was only a lieutenant, he was in complete charge of a group of interrogators, among whom were many with a higher rank than his.

This thug was a specialist in the art of torture. Not for nothing had Goglidze promoted him so rapidly. Ozirsky's strategy was to conduct the psychological attack first, to overwhelm the prisoner with the mass of evidence against him. On his desk lay all the dispatches, letters, and telegrams I had sent to the Jewish Anti-Fascist Committee in my capacity as Birobidzhan correspondent. On one occasion he bragged to me that in preparation for my case he had read as many as thirty books on Jews and the Jewish problem. Judging from the way he conducted the interrogation, I was convinced only of his boundless ignorance. He had memorized a quotation from the works of Alfred Rosenberg, the Nazi ideologue, that "Jews have two Fatherlands, Palestine and Birobidzhan," and he repeated this at every opportunity.

One Yiddish writer, desperate to get even with his tormentor, once offered to help Ozirsky compose a special report proving that Sholom Aleichem was nothing but a talentless scribbler, hoping in this way to expose Ozirsky's ignorance to the more enlightened Soviet authorities. This special report on Sholom Aleichem might have served its purpose had not one of Ozirsky's aides smelled something fishy and squelched it.

Ozirsky never mentioned the name of a Jewish writer without adding some vile epithet. His favorite was *vrag naroda*—"enemy of the people." Itzik Fefer, enemy of the people. Peretz Markish, enemy of the people. Or that "son of a bitch, that nationalist Solomon Mikhoels."

Several times I challenged something he said and showed him up for the ignoramus he was, in return for which he threw me into the hole. Four times, for five days at a stretch, I lay in that dark, disgusting pit, existing on three hundred grams of bread and one glass of water a day. That I did not let the interrogation take the course he wanted was not due to any particular heroism on my part but to the fury this satrap aroused in me by his fiendish baiting. What no other investigator had dared do became a challenge to him—he was going to prove I was an imperialist spy.

According to his research, I wrote my news stories about Birobidzhan in such a way that a foreign espionage agency was able to make use of them.

"Isn't that what you have a counterespionage agency for—to decipher codes?"

"You were too clever for us," he grinned.

At one session Ozirsky pulled a large envelope out of his safe and shoved it at me. "You recognize this?"

I certainly did! I could not keep the surprise out of my face. Because of this envelope the entire Birobidzhan postal system once was turned upside down. This was the story. The Moscow Yiddish newspaper *Eynikayt* had assigned me to do a two-page article entitled, "A Competition between Two Cities." The city of Birobidzhan was then engaged in a socialist competition with Blagoveshchensk, another Far Eastern city. On the basis of the statistics and especially the landscaping of the terrain, Birobidzhan won this contest hands down. Birobidzhan was outstanding in that part of the country for its tree-lined avenues and beautiful flowerbeds, a distinction due in large measure to the work of a Jewish landscape artist named Stein, who had come to Birobidzhan from America in the early 1930s.

As a journalist I wanted to see the competing city for myself, so I went to Blagoveshchensk, which is on the Manchurian border, separated from Sakhalin by the Amur River. I took pictures of the city and interviewed the mayor and several of his staff, as I had done in Birobidzhan. I put the article and the photographs in a large envelope and sent it by airmail to *Eynikayt* in Moscow.

They never received it.

I sent off a telegram to the postmaster, who instituted a search all along the line, including the post office in Birobidzhan and wherever the plane made stops between Khabarovsk and Moscow.

Now this missing envelope turns up on the desk of my interrogator, who sat there flipping the pages without being able to read a word of the article (it was written in Yiddish, of course), but who nevertheless had the triumphant air of a detective who has just caught the world's master spy red-handed.

"You see, Emiot, you can't hide a damn thing from us! And don't tell me about the Soviet constitution and the privacy of the mails! The NKVD stands above all that nonsense!" He pulled out one of the photos. "You took pictures of restricted areas!"

"A park is a restricted area?" I asked naively. How foolish I was then, seeking justice and fairness from the likes of Ozirsky. All he did was add a new charge to my indictment: conspiracy to conduct counterrevolutionary activity.

Of the seven men with whom I was supposed to be in conspiratorial association, there were a couple I had never met or had nothing in common with. But Ozirsky's logic could arrive at any deductions he needed.

"You had connections with certain people. They had connections with other people, whom you may or may not have known. That constitutes a group!"

The period during which Ozirsky had me in his clutches took a heavy toll on my physical and mental health. A Yiddish writer whom I met later in a prison camp told me that he too had been tortured by Ozirsky. This man had undergone a gall-bladder operation shortly before his arrest. The incision had not even healed yet. At one of the sessions, Ozirsky, who of course knew about the man's condition, kicked him the stomach. Another writer, an older man, once told me tearfully how an interrogator had tried to degrade him by abusing him sexually.

The torture assumed various guises. Ozirsky's specialty was psychology. He did not allow his victims to get enough sleep. He deprived them of daily exercise privileges in the prison yard. He resorted often to the punishment cell and its giant rats, where until you learned to overcome your repugnance to these creatures, you ran around in the dark hole like a lunatic. Under Ozirsky's tutelage I learned to feed them out of my hand, sharing with them my daily ration of bread.

I also learned not to attack my tormentor like an enraged tiger, as I had done the first time when he let me rot for five days and nights in the hole and then, as he offered me a tableful of delicacies, said unctuously, "Well, Emiot, how long must we go on fighting each other like this? All you need to do is confess and we'll be friends!"

During one nighttime interrogation he picked up the telephone and called one of his girlfriends. He chatted with her at length and then hung up and called another one. Exhausted from lack of sleep, I begged him to have the guard take me back to my cell.

"You'll do all your resting after the trial—in your grave!"

I sprang at him with my fists, but he pointed his gun at me. The guard pinned my arms from behind. I made up my mind that instant: one way or another, I would never sit at one of Ozirsky's interrogations again.

Obtaining my freedom from Ozirsky cost me dearly. Several times I wrote to the chief of the Investigative Section requesting another interrogator. Nothing happened. I was desperate, unnerved, and sick. My body hurt all over. I went on a hunger strike for two days. The guard summoned the warden, who warned me, "We don't stand for those kinds of games here! If you don't eat anything tomorrow we'll stick a tube up your nose and feed you that way!"

The nurse at the infirmary gave me a tranquilizer and promised to call the prison doctor. After a few reminders, the doctor came.

"What's your problem?"

"I want only one thing: to be assigned to another interrogator, anyone but Ozirsky. And one other little favor. Get me into a cell where I'll have another human being to talk to. Otherwise I'll die of loneliness."

The prison doctor—she had the rank of major—wore the insignia of the MGB on her white uniform. She was supposed to provide medical care for the prisoners, but her care was like the cold water they splash on an unconscious victim to get him ready for the next question.

One day I heard her voice in the corridor. Footsteps running back and forth. Something out of the ordinary was happening. Weeks later I learned that a prisoner had committed suicide in his cell. Shortly thereafter they placed me in that same cell. There were still bloodstains on the scrubbed floor.

I became obsessed with the idea of killing myself. This was easier said than done. The peephole in the door opened regularly, and the guard watched my every movement. I had no metal objects in my cell. Even the buttons on my clothing had been removed. But I kept watching for an opportunity. One day while the guard was busy handing out food I managed to break a piece of glass out of the window in my cell. I tried to locate a vein in my arm but kept cutting only into flesh. Although blood spurted out, I was really in no danger. As if by intuition, the guard returned immediately to my cell. He rushed in, knocked the piece of glass from my hand, and sent out an alarm for the doctor and the warden.

They were of course not so much concerned about saving my life as they were about saving their jobs. The prison must keep the inmates alive until the interrogation is completed. Too many suicide attempts are a black mark against the prison administration: you can't interrogate a dead person. So they bandaged my arm, and the next day I was in a cell for two people.

My first cellmate

Even before I had a chance to look around at my new home, the iron door opened again and there stood my new cellmate.

"*Zdrastvoyitye!* How do you do?"

A pale, haggard face with dark, burning eyes and the delicate features of an old-time yeshiva boy. If you stuck a pair of earlocks on him and put a beaver hat on his head, you'd have a copy of Chanan, the student in Ansky's *Dybbuk*. But this was no yeshiva boy. He was a Russian sailor of about twenty-two. We were together for only a week. On that first day, in my hunger for human company, I told him everything I had experienced in the past several months. (As a rule, prisoners were not kept together in one cell for very long, lest they get to know each other too well and have an opportunity to compare notes and plan a strategy.)

My cellmate was no greenhorn. This was his third prison since his arrest a year earlier in Vladivostok. He was well versed in the prison techniques and could use the "wall telegraph" expertly, so he was able to tell me about several of my friends from Birobidzhan who were also in this prison and whose whereabouts I had not known. Evidently we all had been arrested at the same time.

"At least finally you'll be rid of that bastard Ozirsky," he assured me. "They'll give you another interrogator, because they don't like suicides. They still need you alive for the investigation."

He was just returning from his interrogation and was ravenous as a wolf. I handed him my entire ration of bread, which I hadn't been eating because I was depressed. Although he'd had a few thousand rubles on him at the time of his arrest, the only one allowed to handle that money was his interrogator. Without official permission, inmates were not allowed to buy anything in the prison commissary, not even a pack of cigarettes.

My cellmate had an unusual story. He was one of a crew of seventeen sailors on a gunboat who were accused of having planned a mutiny, including killing the captain and sailing from Port Arthur to nearby Dairen, which no longer belonged to the Soviet Union. The sailors in fact had talked about this among themselves, but they never had worked out a plan to carry it off. They all liked their captain, who was a kind, mild-mannered man, so they dropped the whole idea.

One of the sailors, however, was apparently an informer. A year later the NKVD knew all about it. So the group—among them several members of the Young Communist League—were arrested and charged under article 58, 1-B, military treason, which carries with it a possible death sentence. They were also charged with section 11, conspiracy, which makes that penalty even more certain. In addition, the young sailor in my cell was charged with section 10, dissemination of anti-Soviet propaganda.

How does a member of the Young Communist League, brought up in the Soviet spirit, a graduate of a Soviet naval academy, get mixed up with such counterrevolutionary propaganda?

This was his story. After several years of service in the Pacific, one of the crew—let's call him Shutkov—was given a leave to go home to his village somewhere in Byelorussia. His father had died. His mother, a member of a collective farm, supported herself and several small children. Visiting the collective farm, Shutkov saw with his now more mature eyes the horrible conditions under which the farmers lived and worked.

For a day's backbreaking labor they were paid two hundred grams of bread plus a few potatoes and some cabbage. Government taxes were inordinately high. His sixteen-year-old sister, who wished to move to the city and work in a factory, was not granted permission to do so.

In short, the collective farmer was enslaved to his kolkhoz just as the medieval serf had been enslaved to his squire's estate. Shutkov went to Moscow to tell President Shvernik personally about the intolerable conditions on the collective farms. Of course, he was not permitted to get anywhere near the president.

Shutkov returned to his ship a changed man. The degrading conditions on his mother's collective farm gnawed at his conscience and forced him to raise certain questions about Stalin, "the great father and teacher of the peoples." From that time on, he and some of his shipmates went into the subject more and more deeply. Their minds became more critical. My cellmate, intelligent and inquisitive, no longer believing what he read in the Soviet press, began listening to foreign radio broadcasts in the Russian language. Later the young sailors began discussing ways to escape to Dairen with their gunboat, but it never went beyond the discussion stage.

With another human being in my cell, my own situation improved. The continual solitude had driven me to the point where my sick mind was beginning to transform my innocent cot into images of familiar people. The constant thinking and talking to myself was having an effect on my sanity.

In the meantime, I was not being called for interrogation. The minor wound I had inflicted on myself was slowly heading and was no longer painful. I began feeling much better. The sailor was a pleasant companion. He knew all of *Eugene Onegin* by heart and was happy to recite the poem for me. He had read many Russian novels and remembered some of them well enough to tell me the stories. Having become a student of Soviet law, he explained to me the salient points of my case, as well as the sly tricks of my interrogators.

"Any day now," he advised me, "they'll call you again. In the meantime, they're allowing you a brief rest. But they'll never put you in a cell by yourself again. They'll keep moving you around, and you'll meet some interesting people. You won't feel as depressed or as hopeless as you were in solitary."

He taught me the Morse Code and how to use it in the wall telegraph. He showed me how to make fire by rubbing cotton on the stone floor, as well as other useful things without which a prisoner couldn't survive for very long.

He was correct about the resumption of my interrogation. It began all over again in earnest and went on endlessly. This time the regimen was enforced strictly, with frequent psychological tricks, with five interrogators at one time, and with confrontations with "witnesses" who confirmed my nationalist convictions. These confrontations turned out to be very sad affairs, not so much for me as for the witnesses, who quite often would start sobbing and try to withdraw their previous testimony. Then the interrogator would threaten them with the penalty for perjury, and their testimony remained in the record.

As the sailor had predicted, they never again put me into a cell alone. Before I had a chance to become accustomed to any one particular cell, they were moving me to a second and a third.

Despite the tragedy, suffering, and hopelessness, you slowly settle into the routine of prison life. You are among other people. During your free time you talk, you hear about a host of different experiences, you make observations, and you recognize various kinds of personalities among your fellow inmates. We communicated with our neighbors through the wall and learned about the status of their cases. We even learned how to cope with the "informers' plague." As soon as one of these miserable wretches was exposed anywhere in the prison, the telegraph got busy and all the inmates knew about it before the authorities could make use of him again.

One Yiddish poet, three Japanese generals, and a Russian thief

My interrogators finally realized that the charge of espionage that Ozirsky wanted to pin on me could not be made to stick even under Soviet law, not so much because I refused to knuckle under but because after such a long and exhaustive investigation they still had neither the slightest bit of evidence nor even one trustworthy witness against me. That I would come to trial anyway I saw very clearly, despite the fact that the interrogators had eased up a little. What was now considered established, therefore, was my "Jewish nationalism." I kept insisting that nothing I had done was a crime under article 58, but was rather my duty in my job as a journalist. Still, they continued to press me on that point.

The investigation held, for example, that I had defamed the Soviet Ukraine by alleging that anti-Semitism still existed there. "It is an obvious impossibility that there should be anti-Semitism in the Ukraine," objected my interrogator, "since it is now under Soviet rule."

Every interrogation session now resulted only in new variations on an old theme. They had found another one of my poems, another article I had written, another dispatch—all of a "nationalistic nature."

The translator of my poems, a captain in the MGB, was a Jew who had returned to Birobidzhan from the front. After trying his hand unsuccessfully in the literary field, he had become a loyal employee of the MGB. He asked me cynically whether I found his Russian translation of my poems satisfactory. In his opinion, he smirked, no poet could wish for a better rendering of his work. I already had learned to swallow such bitter pills without gagging. I was no longer surprised when they showed me the findings of the special literary commission organized by the MGB from among the Khabarovsk Russian writers. This commission "found"—on the basis of the literary materials supplied to them—that everything the Birobidzhan Yiddish writers had written was bourgeois nationalist. Such commissions (I learned later) were also set up in Kiev, Minsk, and Moscow. The MGB still had hopes of providing this literary pogrom with a clean facade, and for this they needed the approval of other writers. Needless to say, it was fear and terror that forced the writers to do the MGB's dirty work.

So, having become familiar with the MGB's methods during the long months of my interrogation, it did not surprise me when they read to me from the "confession" of Der Nister, that saintly Yiddish writer, "Yes, I am the master Jewish nationalist."

By studying the habits of the guards, we got to know how you sometimes could outwit one long enough to catch a quick nap during the day. For example, while playing dominoes, we would change seats so that one of us at a time would sit with his back to the peephole, and in that position we would close our eyes for five or ten minutes. But they did manage to prevent us from becoming too friendly. They simply kept moving us around from cell to cell.

One time they transferred me to a large, roomy cell with five bunks. As I entered I counted three Japanese generals in uniform. The oldest, a short, stocky man with a white goatee, asked me in German where I came from. First he bowed and introduced himself: General Usurufu. Then he introduced his two colleagues, a lieutenant general in the artillery and a major general in the air corps. General Usurufu for a long time had been the Japanese military attaché in Berlin. He spoke fluent German, was a rather friendly sort, and on the first day told me his whole story.

During the war he had been deputy commander under General Yamota of the well-known Kwantung Army, which was stationed on the Manchurian-Soviet border. With the defeat of Japan, many Japanese generals were taken prisoner by the Soviets. They were kept in a special prisoner-of-war camp in Khabarovsk, where conditions were tolerable for them and where their food was in keeping with their rank. They also had a more lenient regimen: they were allowed to sleep during the day, they were not required to make up their own beds or clean their own cell, they did not have to empty their own latrine buckets, they did not have to scour their bunks. General Yamota himself was given special quarters and his own guard.

But suddenly the Vaccine Trial began in Khabarovsk against those generals who, during the war, were alleged to have organized the production of poison gas for eventual use in chemical warfare. The seventeen Japanese officers, with General Yamota at their head, were now considered not prisoners of war but war criminals.

The three generals and I were on friendly terms. We played dominoes and checkers. They fashioned a set of chessmen out of bread and we played for hours. Since the two younger generals spoke only Japanese and English, General Usurufu acted as interpreter.

Usurufu told me he had also been charged with the massacre of Soviet partisans in the city of Chita during the Japanese intervention in the Far East during the 1920s. "I was only a soldier obeying orders," he pleaded. "Why blame me?" I deliberately avoided a reply to his question. In this place we were all prisoners and we were all considered criminals.

The general entertained me with elaborate descriptions of his beautiful home in Tokyo, with its staff of twenty servants. He was proud of his sons, who were also high-ranking officers in the Japanese armed forces.

This tranquil life in our cell was rudely shattered by the addition of a fifth man, Volodya, the leader of a gang of thieves in Khabarovsk. Big, strong, and smart, he arrived in a fashionable blue suit and patent-leather shoes. As he entered the cell he introduced himself, but only to me. "Volodya, a Russian. And what the hell are these goddamn Samurai Fascists doing here?"

From my later conversations with him I learned that his brother, a colonel in the Soviet army, had been killed in 1938 during a battle with the Japanese near Lake Khasan. Understandably, he had no love for the Japanese and did everything he could to make life miserable for the generals in our cell.

Volodya had no hesitation about telling me the story of his life. He lost his father at the age of thirteen. He made friends with several other homeless boys. They hung around the railroad stations, picking pockets to survive. Now and then he was caught and served time in rehabilitation homes and prison camps for juvenile offenders. When he grew a little older he became disenchanted with the life of an ordinary pickpocket and tried his hand at riskier but more lucrative jobs. To establish a cover for his nighttime profession, he worked during the day as a lathe operator in a furniture factory, where his work was so exemplary that he was promoted to brigade leader. But he proved even more skillful in his night job as leader of a gang. In a few years they successfully burglarized a long list of jewelry establishments, banks, warehouses, and similar enterprises.

"We worked more with our brains than our muscles. We never took unnecessary risks. We're honest thieves, and we don't like bloodshed. Knocking out a watchman is no big deal for us, but it's nothing to brag about either. It's a lot harder to pull off a job without hurting anybody, but to do it that way you've got to know your business. For instance, instead of hitting a watchman over the head, you either have to doubletalk him or buy him off. You have to be able to sneak into a store and hide there till they close. You have to know how to crack a safe without making too much racket. Whatever you do, you have to do it right the first time. You don't get a second chance."

That was Volodya. His day job in the factory gave him a perfect front. No member of his gang who got caught ever betrayed his friends. In the first place, he knew it would mean the end for him. In the second place, he knew he was not alone—his friends on the outside would help him in whatever way they could while he was on the inside. The Khabarovsk police knew all about this gang and its leader, but they were never able to come up with enough hard evidence to bring Volodya to trial. They finally arranged to frame him.

On March 8, when the Soviet Union marks International Women's Day, Volodya decided to celebrate the holiday with some women workers in the Khabarovsk port. This was the opportunity the police had been waiting for. They sent in one of their own girls, who had a good time with Volodya first and then filed a complaint alleging he had got her drunk and raped her.

Volodya had his alibi ready. One of his own girls testified that on the date in question he had spent all day and all night with her. It also happened that one of his gang let something slip during his interrogation that could have done Volodya in. All Volodya needed was a moment's eye-to-eye confrontation with him, and the guy snatched his report out of the interrogator's hand and tore it to bits.

"We don't play around," Volodya explained to me. "The prosecutor himself is scared to death of us. My interrogator's voice shook when he asked me if it was really true that thieves get even with those who send them up. I told him yes, it certainly was, we skin people like that alive. You should've seen the bastard! He turned pale as a peeled potato!"

Everybody in the prison administration had a lot of respect for Volodya. For example, when a package comes for a prisoner from the outside, everything in it is broken apart and inspected from top to bottom. Even a loaf of bread is sliced up just in case something has been baked into it that could be useful for the inmate. Volodya's packages, however, were delivered to him virtually untouched. And if he as much as suspected that they hadn't delivered a package to him immediately, he banged on the cell door and cursed the prison functionaries unto the tenth generation.

Essentially Volodya wasn't a brutish person. He never sat down to eat without sharing with me whatever he received from the outside, although (as he explained to me) it's against the code for a professional thief to eat with a civilian. "But *nitchevo*, you're OK, old man!" The reason I was OK with Volodya is that I passed a certain test with flying colors, and right in his presence. This is what happened.

One day he sent a message to some of the girls in the prison that the following morning he would toss a silk handkerchief to them over the fence around our exercise area. The place where we took our daily walk was a small square, cut into four segments by two intersecting fences and surrounded overall by a high brick wall. The inmates from four cells thus could be let out for their walk at the same time and still be separated by the fences. Volodya tossed the handkerchief over our fence; he did it so skillfully that the guard on the watch tower, although he saw it happen, could not be sure who had done it.

As we were being herded back into our cells, a guard pulled me roughly out of line and cursed at me: "An old fart like you messin' around with them kids!"

I knew the prisoners' code well enough by then not to deny his accusation. The guard ordered me to get ready for solitary. When they called the girls into the warden's office, however, they all swore by their mother's honor that they'd had the handkerchief among them for a long time and that the guard must have a grudge against that old man. To my surprise, I was not punished in any way. Volodya congratulated me proudly on my commendable behavior.

Taking advantage of my newly won esteem, I suggested to Volodya that he try to be a little more cordial to the three Japanese generals. "Prisoners in the same cell should treat each other decently and not try to settle old scores. Isn't that the code?"

"But they're lousy Fascists!"

"Well, with you people I'm a Fascist too, you know. I'm a political, remember?"

"Nah, you're one of our own Fascists. Those bastards are foreign Fascists!"

"And you, Volodya, are you exactly a good Soviet person? That was state property you stole."

"I'm a Soviet person and I'm not against the Soviet system. So I stole a little—who'll ever miss it? Our country is plenty rich."

The three Japanese tried to live in peace with him. They overlooked the dirty names he called them, they treated him to their good cigarettes. But it was no use. He kept thinking up new ways to harass them. One day, while I was playing chess with them, he said to me in Russian, "Watch closely and I'll show you how it's done. I'm not a pickpocket by profession—I don't like to waste my time on such small change—but I still remember a few tricks from the old days."

And he went to work. Whatever the generals had in their pockets migrated to Volodya's. When he was finished, he returned their property to them—at my request. But I could see that beneath their polite, smiling masks their blood was churning over this grave affront to their pride. It was just too much for them to bear. They complained to their interrogator, who called Volodya in and warned him that if he were really such a Soviet patriot he would try to get along with these generals, because their testimony was essential to the investigation. Volodya, however, was unmoved by this approach as well.

"Get those Fascists out of there or move me to another cell!"

"Keep it up and I'll have you in chains!" the warden threatened.

"Go ahead and try it—if you want to leave this place in a box!"

"You're not such a hero in here, big mouth! We've tamed wilder animals than you!"

"One of these days you'll find them with their throats cut—and you'll be responsible, not me."

Volodya made his point. They moved him to another cell. The generals revived right under my eyes, even though the prison authorities grew rougher and rougher on them. With the end of their interrogation came the end of their easy life. They were given the same rations as all the other inmates. No more rice. Only grits or gruel.

General Usurufu turned up his nose. "We feed this garbage to our pigs!" But none of this bothered him so much as the fact that the judge would not allow him to come into court in full military regalia, with his stiff, shiny, yellow boots. "It's a disgrace!" he repeated over and over, unable to accept this humiliation, this insult to his station.

The hearings lasted several days. At the end of each day the generals returned to the cell red-faced and sweating. They lost their appetite. They were attacked by diarrhea and kept apologizing to me every time they used the bucket. General Usurufu neglected my lessons in Japanese. He stopped practicing his Japanese version of chess, which requires exceptional patience and concentration. He grew more and more disconsolate and kept asking me whether a man his age would have to work in the prison camp. The other two officers fell apart completely. Because they were still young, their fate was practically a certainty: a long stretch at hard labor. The only question was how long.

The three generals were sentenced to twenty-five years. If they survived, they most likely were freed later in accordance with the Soviet-Japanese peace treaty. If they are still alive, each of them most certainly remembers the tricks with which Volodya the thief tormented them.

Of Volodya's fate I'm more certain. Before he was transferred from our cell he called me aside. "I'm going to give you a password. Every thief in this prison—if he's an honest man—will honor the code. When they hear that you sat in the same cell with the boss of the Khabarovsk thieves, not only will they leave you alone but they'll make sure nobody else bothers you."

Later, in the Irkutsk transfer camp, I actually did fall afoul of such a gang soon after I arrived. They shoved me into a corner and started removing the shoes right off my feet. I promptly told them with whom I'd had the honor of sharing a cell. The head of the gang immediately found me a good seat and instructed his pals to treat me as one of their own. From him I also learned that Volodya had again beaten the rap. His alibi was airtight, and the police had no other evidence.

Meanwhile, my own troubles were endless. The interrogator who warned me from the start that nobody gets out of this place a free man had not lied. During the year I spent in the investigatory prison, not one person got off without a sentence of some kind. Very few were tried in court. Most were sentenced by a troika—three judges who sat somewhere in Moscow and skimmed through the report sent in by the interrogator with the concurrence of the prosecution. (The latter generally had no opinion of its own; it merely OK'd whatever the organs of the MGB prepared.) Those prisoners already sentenced were kept segregated until a work order arrived from a prison camp. We learned the extent of their punishment from the slips of paper they left in the latrine room or through symbols written on the wall according to a prearranged code. Anything less than a "tenner"—ten years at hard labor—was most unusual.

Less than five years was so rare it was considered a miracle.

Nonetheless, an even greater miracle happened once in the Khabarovsk prison. Instead of the usual document 206, which signified that the prisoner had been found guilty, one of the inmates was given a 204—not guilty! When I later told my fellow inmates in the labor camp about this, the veterans there simply refused to believe it—it was impossible, they said, under Stalin's justice.

But it actually did happen once, as we shall see.

The miracle

Again I was moved into a new cell, this time with two other inmates. One was an experienced locomotive machinist a Russian from Siberia, who had been charged with theft of state property. Because Rail Transport was under the aegis of the political police, he was sent to prison as a political. His case hadn't the slightest connection with politics, however. What had happened was that he was raising some pigs for his own use at a holiday feast, and since there was no fodder available in the government stores, he had to look elsewhere.

It happened that his train regularly passed a big silo where sacks of grain were strewn all around the railroad platform, practically begging to be taken home. So he put a few of them into his locomotive. Unfortunately for him he was caught in the act. For this crime he was given three years, the minimum sentence. The machinist was so agreeably surprised by this light sentence that he decorated all the walls in the latrine room with big 3's.

My second cellmate, whose father was a Georgian and whose mother was a Russian, had a unique story indeed. After graduating from a naval academy, he worked for many years on Soviet ships as a chief mechanic. Since these ships would dock in various Soviet ports, he had three apartments: one in Riga, one in Vladivostok, and one in Voroshilovsk. He was married to a Tatar beauty, and this gorgeous wife of his (he sighed) became the source of all his troubles.

Next door to his home in Vladivostok lived an MGB

interrogator, who coveted his neighbor's young wife and decided to get her husband out of the way. The first thing he did was surround him with an army of spies, who eventually ferreted out the information that this naval officer once had used his high position to buy furniture for one of his apartments at discounted prices.

On the basis of this evidence the interrogator—his name happened to be Goglidze, a fact which is vital to the story—began an official investigation, which resulted in a tenner for my cellmate. This fellow, however, was not your ordinary, run-of-the-mill citizen. Not only was he a Party member, but his father had helped to install Soviet power in Georgia. Even in prison this mechanic knew his way around. As a nonpolitical offender he was not sent to a remote, tough prison camp but was put to work on ships docked for repairs. The sailors on board knew him, and as is the custom among men of the sea, they wouldn't neglect their shipmate just because he was a jailbird. Whenever the mechanic boarded a ship he was wined and dined and supplied with the best of everything. In the meantime, his devoted young wife, who was really very much in love with him, ran from one official to another, turning the world upside down to get her husband released.

All this activity didn't sit well with the interrogator Goglidze. He began digging deeper; perhaps he could find this naval officer actually involved in some political sin. In Russia it is not at all difficult to find that sort of thing, if you look hard enough.

After World War II the chief mechanic served aboard a Soviet ship that sailed to the United States on a goodwill mission. There the crew of his ship arranged a charity ball and invited a lot of people. This was just the kind of event the plotter Goglidze had been waiting for. He accused the officer of having used the occasion as a cover for a meeting with American spies. As proof he offered the fact that the officer, on the journey back to Russia, had been seen reading the Russian émigré press printed in America. Furthermore,

another officer of the same ship had defected to the West, and the chief mechanic, who was also secretary of the Party branch on board ship, had tried to sweep the whole matter under the rug.

They took the chief mechanic out of the camp where he was serving his furniture sentence and transferred him to the Khabarovsk prison for politicals. That's where the miracle happened.

Our naval officer sat down and wrote an appeal to the chief of the Khabarovsk MGB, whose name (you will remember) was also Goglidze, listing his services to the Soviet cause and his own personal and family credentials. At the same time, he also emphasized that the Voroshilovsk interrogator Goglidze was taking advantage of the similarity in their names for the vilest machinations, thus besmirching the good name of Beria's representative in the Far East. He labored mightily for days before he was able to set forth clearly, in the twenty-four pages of his complaint, all the important facts concerning the dastardly conduct of the Voroshilovsk Goglidze.

And although the Khabarovsk Goglidze himself was not a whit more moral than the dissolute womanizer from Voroshilovsk, who thought nothing of ruining a man because he lusted after his pretty wife, and although both Goglidzes were no worse and no better than their boss Beria, still, the complaint of the naval officer went straight to its target—the chief's vanity. The Khabarovsk Goglidze was offended deeply by his namesake's imprudent acts, which easily could have redounded on him, the head of the regional Ministry of State Security. In short, the writer of the complaint was declared innocent of all the political charges against him.

Despite the fact that my cellmate had to return to his camp to complete the remainder of his original sentence, his joy knew no bounds. In those days even the most serious crimes were not punished so severely as those under article 58. To be named a *vrag naroda*, an enemy of the people, meant to lose all hope of ever returning to normal society again.

I don't know what eventually happened with my cellmate, but it's clear that his courageous little wife, the Tatar beauty, saved him from a long captivity. After all, it's not as though he had committed a political crime.

Awaiting trial

From the piles of clean wash in the bathhouse where we were taken every seventh day, I could tell that our prison was filled now to overflowing. Sitting inside the cell you never saw the prisoners; you heard only their footsteps in the corridor. Your ear became ultrasensitive, like a blind person's. It learned to recognize, even to distinguish between different steps. You tried to visualize the appearance of a person from the sound of his tread.

A considerable number of the prisoners were women. They too grew accustomed to living with their misfortune. They even managed to flirt a little with the men behind the iron doors by performing a sort of hop-skip for us as they walked through the corridor. By means of the wall telegraphs we knew who they were and what they had been charged with. Mostly they were young women accused of espionage. The older women, generally from collective farms, had been arrested for anti-Soviet agitation.

A fascinating phenomenon: the attitude of the women prisoners toward the men was extremely compassionate. Often they willingly went hungry themselves and gave their own bread ration to men who needed more food simply to stay alive. This would be arranged either through a rare humane guard or by hiding the bread behind a heater pipe in the toilet room.

My own interrogation was over. I was placed in a large cell to await my summons to trial. Nervous, tense, I paced back and forth, trying to memorize the speech I planned to deliver as my closing statement. The charge of espionage had been dropped, but there were plenty of other charges I would have to refute. I had been accused of organizing a group whose aim was to disseminate nationalistic propaganda by means of the written and spoken word. In wartime, such a crime in the Soviet Union is punishable by death. In peacetime, Soviet law provides a penalty of six months to twenty-five years. The six-month sentence was completely unheard of. My best interrogator admitted to me, "Five years is the lightest sentence in such cases, but it usually is meted out to illiterates without knowledge or education who mutter against something they think is unfair. But an educated man like you is more responsible for what he says and does."

My struggles against the inquisitors and the prosecutors were in vain, as were my repeated declarations that nothing I had done was anti-Soviet and that the entire indictment was not only ludicrous but in direct violation of the Soviet constitution. Hadn't President Kalinin himself described the Jewish Autonomous Region as a place where the national identity of Russian Jewry could and should be preserved?

"Everything has its special time," my interrogator patiently enlightened me. "In our country, policies change frequently. Our dialectical approach is dictated by life itself. What was correct yesterday may be incorrect—even criminal —today."

I was terribly concerned about my forthcoming trial. The group I allegedly organized consisted of (according to the charges) seven people. Only once during the investigation did I see my codefendants. Several of them were in fact my close friends. How they had deteriorated! Haggard, emaciated, as though they had just been through a long and painful illness. Exhausted and broken by the constant questioning, we embraced each other tearfully. Though we were not permitted to speak to each other, we somehow managed to communicate the knowledge that we had all gone through a similar degrading ordeal.

The prosecution read us all the factual proof of our guilt: clippings from newspapers and magazines, reports of literary evenings, speeches we had made to new immigrants, telegrams, letters, and written testimony by informers (we were even told their names). Additionally, in a separate volume (which they did not show us) there were multitudinous reports from the secret agents who had been spying on us all these years. We objected particularly to section 11—that we had formed a secret organization. What kind of secret organization?

It turned out that all the evidence on that point came from a Yiddish writer named S. What in the world did he have to do with us? Well, it seems that S. considered it practically an honor that the investigators had included him in our company and out of gratitude he kept feeding them new statements as the case grew by leaps and bounds to the magnitude they had hoped for in the first place.

Among other things, S. informed them that the Jewish Anti-Fascist Committee had decided to send a special delegation personally to Comrade Stalin to expose the existence of anti-Semitism among the highest Soviet officials in the Kremlin itself. S. explained that this meeting with Stalin had been arranged by Professor Zbarski, the man who had embalmed Lenin's body and who was an intimate friend of Stalin's. (He had received a Stalin Prize for his accomplishment.) For days the interrogator badgered me about this. "It is impossible," he insisted, "that you, who were the correspondent for all of Birobidzhan and who were a confidant of Mikhoels, knew nothing of this plan."

Actually, the first I heard of it was from my interrogator. But that adventurer S. caused us endless heartache with his inexhaustible fabrications. It wasn't until we were both in the prison camp that he explained this plan to me, a story he had invented out of whole cloth. Why had he done it, when he knew that with his incredible accusations he was only dragging more and more innocent people into the mess? Well, that's exactly why he did it, he boasted. He knew that the bigger and more fantastic these libels grew, the quicker the whole business would be exposed! This way the world would find out about it, and there would be such a storm of indignation and protest that the Kremlin would have to pay attention. And that, he said, was the only thing that could save us.

The only thing it did, however, was get us deeper into trouble. We tried to prepare ourselves to attack these charges in the courtroom. But they didn't call us to trial. We sat in separate cells and waited, without hearing a word, as if we no longer existed.

Since I no longer was being called out for interrogation, I had plenty of time to observe my cellmates. They were all young people whose interrogations had been completed. Apparently they were to be tried right here in Khabarovsk, because their indictments already had been filed with the regional court. There were eight of us in the cell, with four beds still empty, but not for long.

Oddly enough, the days went by more or less pleasantly. The young fellows kept up a steady correspondence with the girls in the prison. They described themselves as great heroes and in return they received love notes from the girls. They enumerated their qualities as one does in a matrimonial advertisement. The fellows talked about the girls as if they had known them all their lives. Most of this communication was conducted through the walls, except during our walks in the yard. Then the messages were sent by a special coughing code. Often I wondered if these young people were at all aware of the long years of pain and suffering awaiting them out there in the camps.

A young Ukrainian officer in our cell by the name of Kuzma put on concerts for us. His forte was playing women's roles. Disguised as a woman, he had escaped from a prison two years earlier and gotten as far as Chita. He might have made it all the way to the Ukraine without being caught, had he not been such an incurable showoff. On the train westward he began bragging about how he had given his jailers the slip. Even before he got off the train, he was back in the MGB's clutches.

With him in our cell was also his brother-in-law, a Red Army sergeant, exceptionally handsome and innocent as a babe. It seems that he used to visit his brother-in-law Kuzma to listen to the radio. One evening Kuzma showed him an article in the *Soviet Encyclopedia* about the rich natural resources of the Ukraine. The sergeant asked rhetorically whether the time hadn't come for Ukrainian independence. Unfortunately for him, there happened to be a third person in the room at the time. Since the government already had in its possession factual evidence that Kuzma had tried to smuggle in weapons for the Ukrainian rebels (which he denied), they picked up the handsome sergeant as well.

Particularly bizarre was the accusation against Vladimir, a young engineer in a Khabarovsk factory. When some fellow workers asked him once to come out to a May Day parade, he replied, "We engineers wear smocks at our work. I'm too embarrassed to march in the streets dressed like that."

On the basis of that chance remark, the secret police decided to monitor a few more of his subversive conversations. They got what they were looking for. On one occasion he very recklessly told a friend that his Zeiss camera took better pictures than his Kharkov camera. This was clear evidence that he was "praising foreign technology and denigrating if not defaming Soviet technology," which is a crime under article 58, section 10, point 1. At the very least, this young engineer would get a five-year sentence for his momentary indiscretion.

My sentence

The young fellows in my cell became even busier when the women were transferred to the floor below us, but for me this was the last straw. I had been waiting impatiently for only one thing—my trial. Constantly waiting and thinking about it and pacing around like a madman. But here these young people started making ropes from threads pulled out of their clothes and blankets. What did they do with the ropes? They attached empty matchboxes to them, which they lowered through the window to the floor below. The women prisoners filled the boxes with *makhorka*—an inexpensive tobacco for rolling your own cigarettes—and along with the *makhorka* might come a little note in which someone poured out her heart and soul. Notes about a poor lonely mother whose imprisoned daughter had been the sole breadwinner of the family, or about a child who was left motherless somewhere, or about a budding young life cut down before it had a chance to bloom.

A specialist in composing heart-rendering, poetic replies to these notes was our quiet, good-natured cellmate Vasily, who still wore his linen army uniform with all the insignia stripped off. He was an expert in matching up the pieces of newspaper we found in the food packages sent to us by our families. This requires some explanation. No newspapers were allowed into the prison. Friends and family would send us scraps of newspaper pages ostensibly for rolling our cigarettes. Vasily would assemble all the scraps carefully and put together a news clipping. Then he would read it to us. We were starved for any information about the world outside.

Who can plumb the depths of the Russian soul? This young blond fellow—he wasn't even twenty—already was destined to pay heavily for his sympathies toward the oppressed. This young *Komsomoletz*, who had read nothing except what was OK'd by his military unit, suddenly became deeply concerned about the difficult conditions in the collective farms. During his month's leave he had traveled across an entire province, studying the hard life of those farmers. Then he wrote a long, critical article with his recommendations for radically improving the general conditions on the collective farms, intending to send it to the Central Committee of the Communist Party in Moscow. He put it into an envelope, sealed it, and left it in a drawer.

Apparently someone suspected what he was doing. The envelope was stolen and eventually reached the secret police. Vasily was arrested and questioned. He had no connections with anyone else, he had never shared his thoughts with anyone, and he certainly had not told anyone what he was writing to the Party leaders. Whatever he had written had remained his secret, and only the Politburo in Moscow would have known his ideas and opinions. Nevertheless, he was charged under article 58, and he too was awaiting his trial impatiently. While this could be said of all my cellmates, they meanwhile were passing the time with these truly platonic love affairs.

The day finally arrived when the guard came to the door of our cell and called out my name. Now at last I would have an opportunity to tell my side of the story to a court. All my cellmates wished me well. Vasily embraced and kissed me in the traditional Russian manner. The guards led me through the long, dark, depressing corridors until we reached the warden's office. Here an individual dressed like a court official smiled at me crookedly and handed me a slip of paper.

I had no idea what it was, but after I read a few lines, fiery circles danced before my eyes. This was no summons to appear for a trial! It was the finished product—my sentence. A sentence without a trial!

The document informed that under sections 10 and 11 of article 58 I had been sentenced to ten years at hard labor.

I barely managed to control my voice sufficiently to ask the flunky, "Where is the court? Who tried me?"

"Take it easy," he said. "Read it again."

I was indeed bewildered. As soon as I had seen the words "ten years" I could read no further. When I looked more closely I saw that I had been tried in Moscow by a special military court of the MGB—behind closed doors and in absentia.

"It could have been worse, you know," the official with the hypocritical smile consoled me. "If they had tried you here, and if you'd had a defense lawyer, your sentence would have been much stiffer. You're lucky they tried you in absentia. In such cases they always hand out lighter sentences."

"But I didn't ask for this kind of trial! I was ready to defend—"

He cut me short. He had no time now to discuss this with me. He still had to deliver his slips of paper to the other defendants.

When the guard took me back to the cell I was still shaking my head and seething inside. My cellmates, however, envied me. "At least now you know where you stand. In our case, we're still neither here nor there." Especially sympathetic were the Ukrainians. "For advocating Ukrainian independence they now give you twenty-five years. Maybe we'll be lucky too. If they give us the same kind of trial, maybe we'll also get off with a tenner."

For me this was hardly a consolation. The taste in my mouth was bitter as gall. Ten years! Ten years! Almost mechanically my head began to translate that into days, into hours. There are 365 days in a year. Ten times 365 is 3,650.

Hard labor for 3,650 days! How would I ever endure it? Would I ever be a free man again? Would I ever see my family again? My heart and spirit were broken, my body worn and spent, my resistance at its lowest ebb—except for my tears, which flowed as if they would never stop again as long as I lived.

From veteran prisoners of the labor camps I had learned about the inhuman conditions there, about the brutal guards whose sole function was to make life miserable for all the prisoners but especially for politicals. In our cell there was a kindly old veterinarian who had served one tenner and been arrested for the second time because "the horses entrusted to my care insisted on dropping dead." He said to me sympathetically, "I don't like to tell you this, but it's better to know it beforehand. Life will be very hard for you there. You're not very strong physically, which is bad enough, but aside from that, you're not accustomed to the backbreaking work they'll make you do. And on top of all that, there's no lack of Jew-haters in those places."

My only consolation was that I no longer had to worry about memorizing my defense speech. Somewhere I needed to find the courage and endurance to face whatever the future held for me—the long hot journey in the locked and guarded trains, the transit camps along the way before I reached the final destination. And who knows where that would be? Here they tell you nothing at all. Except to wait. Sit and wait for that work requisition from the camp.

On the road to penal servitude

It was a hot July day. We had stripped down to our underwear. The cigarette smoke in the cell befouled the already fetid air. The conversation sagged. The young Ukrainians weren't even swapping their dirty jokes. Hot and exhausted, we lay in our bunks lethargically and dozed.

The sudden loud banging on the cell door reminded us that sleeping was not permitted during the day. Ivan began dreaming out loud about his village by the Volga, where he used to swim every day. Oh the river, the river! There was nothing he missed more than that river, not even the girls who used to dance to the music of his accordion. Especially that Katya—how pretty she was, with her eyes blue as cornflowers. He went into ecstatic descriptions of the Volga—how it looked in the daylight, a solid piece of molten silver, and how it looked at sundown, when the silver turned to gold. What he wouldn't give now for a swim in the clear, fresh waters of the Volga River!

And here in our cell the air was thick enough to cut. The fifteen-minute walk outdoors was only enough to whet the appetite for more. Still, each of us was hoping the same thing—that they not move us anywhere during these torrid days. Hot as it was in the cell, in the convoy trains it would be even worse. Here at least we had cold water to drink whenever we wished, and as much as we wished, and we could walk around in our underwear and dream about a river with fresh, flowing water.

On one of these sultry days the iron door opened unexpectedly. In walked a young lieutenant of the guard. He threw a hard look at me and snapped, "Bring your things and follow me!" This meant that I wouldn't be coming back to this cell anymore. But they weren't moving me to another one. My requisition from the camp had finally arrived.

In the prison lobby my wooden suitcase was waiting for me, along with a package of my underwear and shirts, which had been locked up all year in the cellar. Also waiting for me was a convoy guard, to whom I was turned over by the prison administrator. They handed me a large sealed envelope containing my dossier and a summary of my case, along with a little sack of food for five days—bread, salted fish, and some sugar. My new guard searched the suitcase and removed my clock. Prisoners are not supposed to know what time of day it is. Such information can only be useful for escape plans. Finally he gave the command: *"Poydyom!* Move!"

I marched in front of him with my suitcase in one hand and the sack in the other until we reached the center of the main yard, where a van was waiting, loaded with prisoners. This vehicle did not have separate cubicles; we were all crammed in together, men and women. During the ride the convoy guard stood in a corner, apart from the prisoners.

Sitting next to me and crying her heart out was a pretty young girl who had been brought from the criminals' jail. Tearfully she told me about her twenty-five year sentence for embezzling funds that belonged to a government enterprise. She raised her hands desperately to heaven: "O dear God! I have lived so little in Your world!"

Not all the prisoners in the van took their fate so seriously. Some of them were singing so loudly the guard had to shut them up. For these criminal offenders the transfer from one prison or camp to another had become a break in the monotony. It gave them an opportunity to have a little fun with the women prisoners, telling their bawdy stories and putting their tattoed arms around the young girls, who squealed like piglets on their way to market.

Eventually we arrived at the railroad station, where four Stolypin cars stood ready for us. These trains, named after a czarist minister of the interior, had barred windows and compartments closed off by a grating. The guard pushed me into one of the cars that already was packed to the limit. The trains had been crawling along like this from far-off Vladivostok, taking on more and more prisoners from points all along the route. All the seats in my compartment were taken, even the upper bunks. I glanced around at my neighbors: typical criminals, half-naked in their striped sailor shirts that were almost a uniform with them. They were initiating a greenhorn political, a well-dressed man with an expensive-looking valise. The man resisted and threatened to call the guard, but it wouldn't have done him any good. Although we knew they were close by at all times, the guards kept out of sight. Meanwhile my neighbor had been relieved of his shirts and suits and had been given a dozen or more punches in the ribs besides.

I sat on my battered suitcase, not even thinking about the shabby clothes inside it. They were taking my life away— why fight over a few old shirts? I knew from my prison experience that where the criminal offenders make up the majority they will do whatever they have a mind to. I wondered whether I would last long enough to reach the transit camp. It was so airless in the car you couldn't even strike a match.

When the tongues of the prisoners loosened up a bit I learned I was on a train with a shipment of hardened jailbirds. Their leader was not merely a thief but a *mokrishka*, a killer who boasted that in order to get the fancy jacket he was wearing he'd had to kill a young boy. He first had asked the boy nicely to give up the garment, but when his victim refused and started calling for help, what choice did he have? A *mokrishka* got his kicks from shedding a little blood during a robbery. Even his peers hated his guts.

Another prisoner in the car, with a scarred face and one blind eye, apparently had a reputation for cold-bloodedness. An old bandit of about sixty, he had served time in many jails. Now he was being transferred from Kamchatka, where he had been serving a twenty-five-year sentence for robbery and murder. (Capital punishment had been abolished in Russia at that time; death sentences were commuted to twenty-five years.) This brute sat and entertained his fellow passengers with tales of his killings in the same detached way one would describe the routine of an everyday chore.

These two hardened criminals were the center of attraction for the others in the compartment, especially the youthful offenders, who had been arrested for running away from vocational schools and given six months to a year in a prison camp. On the train they waited on the regulars hand and foot like servants.

The meals on these Stolypin cars consisted of a slice of bread and a piece of salted herring. We drank a lot of water and had to use the toilet frequently, which meant inconveniencing the guards. In this respect the politicals were second-class citizens—the guards simply refused to take us to the latrine car. (Later we learned that the guards and the criminals were in a kind of partnership: the property stolen from the politicals was sold at the stations along the line, and the guards shared the profits.) We soon came up with a way of handling this particular problem. The politicals made a deal with the criminals to allow them to urinate in their own boots, which were later given to the thieves in return for services rendered.

I was liberated of my belongings quickly and rather painlessly. When I returned from my first trip to the latrine, my suitcase was practically empty. But since I didn't say anything, my traveling companions gave me their old cast-off rags in exchange and let me keep one suit so I wouldn't have to walk around naked.

"If you play ball with us," the one-eyed bandit told me,

"and don't holler bloody murder about every little thing, we'll get along just fine."

I felt particularly sorry for one elderly political from Vladivostok. The old man had a bad case of diarrhea, and although he swallowed nothing during the whole trip except the hot water and hard biscuit that was distributed to us once a day, he suffered from continual stomach cramps. In the infirmary car they gave him some powders for his condition, but since he had no fever, they refused to move him into sickbay. The old man, not permitted to use the latrine, finally had to relieve himself right on the floor beneath him. After a couple of days, the criminals raised such a fuss about the stench that the guards had to move him out.

In the meantime the train dragged its wretched cargo through endless stretches of forest, stopping from time to time at a station platform, where from the bottom of our loathsome abyss we sometimes could catch a glimpse of freedom through the barred windows.

The prison train has stopped. Across from it stands a passenger train with first-class sleeping compartments. On the platform you can see the freshly shaven, neatly combed, well-rested, well-fed, sturdily built citizens in their perfectly fitting suits. Beside them are their smiling, coquettish ladies. They are sightseeing. The men show off their worldliness, pointing knowingly here and there, explaining things to the women, who mince about the platform carefree as birds. Why don't they take any notice of the barred prison cars? Why doesn't it occur to them that tomorrow or the next day any one of them could be riding on this train to an unknown destination?

On the eighth day we stopped at the transit point in Taishet. Exactly midway between Moscow and Vladivostok in eastern Siberia, Taishet is a name that strikes terror in the hearts of Soviet prisoners. Taishet signifies not only the place itself—although in this sprawling city alone, with its wooden houses and wooden sidewalks, there are a dozen or so prison camps—but the entire Taishetlag, a system of labor camps that stretches for hundreds of kilometers. The first camps were built by the prisoners incarcerated there in 1937–38, the years of the *Yezhovtshina*, under that infamous hangman Nikolai Ivanovich Yezhov, People's Commissar of Internal Affairs.

Later, Japanese war prisoners were sent here. It was they who extended the railway line from Taishet to Lena. All that's left of them are cemeteries. The Japanese, accustomed to a moderate climate, dropped like flies in the Siberian frost. Eventually this became a closed camp, that is, a maximum-security camp with an extremely rigorous regimen. To the designation of every camp section is appended a zero—041, 023, etc.—and that little cipher symbolizes the curse of isolation and penal servitude. The regimen in those camps is similar to a maximum-security prison, except that the inmates don't wear shackles on their feet. They work ten hours a day at hard labor and are paid nothing except the food they eat. From ten in the evening to six in the morning the entire area is sealed tight. The prisoners wear numbers on their shirts and pants and may send letters out to their families—and only their families—no more than twice a year.

In the transfer point at Taishet, however, the regimen is somewhat easier. Whether because it is close to a railway line and the authorities are afraid of a prison break, or because new prisoners are arriving here constantly, among whom are lifers en route to other camps—whatever the reason, conditions here are not as bad as in a closed camp.

On the other hand, the guards here are worse. Transferring prisoners from the railroad station to the camp in open trucks over a primitive, bumpy road, the guards are quick to use their rifle butts on prisoners' hands, even if they are only holding onto the sides of the vehicle. The guards make that half-hour trip so unbearable you're glad to reach the camp, where you can at least breathe a little easier, although you have to wait here a long time in the awful heat without a drop of water.

Encircling the camp is a high, wooden fence topped with several rows of barbed wire. To make doubly sure this is not used as an escape route, the two meters closest to the fence are strictly off limits, and the guards in the watchtowers have orders to shoot any prisoner they catch there. Nonetheless, overhead is the blue sky, and the air you breathe is fresh and clean.

When I arrived at Taishet the place was jammed with prisoners awaiting transfer. All the bunks were occupied, so we slept on the floor. I was assigned to a work brigade led by an Armenian, a clever, crafty man but not a vicious one. He oriented us to the camp rules and regulations, as well as the rights and duties of the brigade leader. We are in this place only temporarily, he told us, but even here we are expected to do a certain amount of work. We will be given a physical examination and assigned to either category 1 or category 2. A few of us will be placed in the invalid category. In the latter case, the prisoner may end up in an easy camp, where the work is not so punitive. Meanwhile, we must obey the orders of our brigadier at all times.

Since there was no work for us to do during the first couple of days, I wandered around the camp, observing the prisoners, talking with them and getting the news. News is what I was yearning for after a year of isolation from the rest of the world. The most important thing was that here I met other Jews. In the Khabarovsk prison too there must have been other Jews beside the Birobidzhaners, but they never were placed in the same cells with us. Undoubtedly this was a deliberate policy. During that entire year I had only one Jewish cellmate, a man from Komsomolsk. An assimilated Jew who didn't know a word of Yiddish or Hebrew, he still was arrested for Jewish nationalism when he spoke out against anti-Semites in his factory. He was in my cell for only a very short time before our jailers discovered their error and moved him. In Taishet there were a great many Jews, most of them from Moscow.

The women at this transfer point were separated from the men by a fence, but they ate in the same mess hall with us and worked together with us. Most of them had been charged with helping the Ukrainian nationalist movement.

There were many veteran prisoners here en route from one camp to another. At the Taishet transfer point their files were checked and brought up to date. Prisoners were also brought here for new interrogations. There were victims here of the Zhukov trials, high military officers whose only crime consisted in their recognition of Marshal Georgi Zhukov (and not Stalin) as the real hero of the Soviet victory over Nazi Germany. Our infirmary nurse, for example, was the wife of Zhukov's adjutant. She and her husband both had been sentenced for taking part in a rebellion against the "great father and teacher of the peoples." Here I also met people of various religious sects, particularly Jehovah's Witnesses, who all had been sentenced for cooperating with foreign capitalism.

From other inmates I learned the full extent of the Jewish arrests that had taken place throughout the Soviet Union in late 1948. Of two thousand prisoners in transit at Taishet, one-third were Jews.

The camp was dirty and crowded, the living quarters abominable, but still I found it interesting. I remember one day suddenly recalling Dostoevski's strange story, "Happiness: The First Emotion on Hearing That a Friend Has Suddenly Died." I always had been repelled by this paradox. But here we were, inhumanly abused, our minds disoriented; it was true that the innate sense of curiosity becomes a sort of joy of discovery. I spoke with many people. New lives unfolded before me, new experiences, horrible experiences, but so different from my own! Apparently this is sufficient reason for feeling a kind of pleasure in having crossed into an unfamiliar world, just as, when we were children, we loved to play inside the tables that Mother had turned upside down in the yard when she scrubbed the floors in the house.

How painful those new experiences were for us new-comers!

They took us out for the first time to work in the camp, men and women packed into an open truck. In order that the prisoners not be catapulted out during the bumpy ride, we were shackled to each other hand and foot. Our job was to tear down an old building and sort out the material into logs, boards, bricks, and so forth. I had not yet learned about the local gnats, which breed there by the millions. I rolled up my sleeves and fell to work; after all, it would be a disgrace to do less than the women prisoners, who lugged seven or eight bricks at a time or carried big logs in tandem. By the end of the shift, my arms were so swollen from insect bites that I had to go to the infirmary, where the nurse smeared my arms with ointment and wrapped them in bandages.

Upon arrival at the transfer point, each prisoner listed his occupation. The rumor was that a professional had a better chance of remaining at the transfer point for a longer period of time. Those who were brought here from the more remote camps warned us that conditions out there were incredibly bad. The air was filled with gnats all day long, the bread ration was hardly enough to keep you alive, and the camp overseers were all sadists. To remain at the transfer point a little while longer was a blessing.

When finally I was called for my physical examination, the doctor, a young woman, did not acknowledge any of my complaints except for the cataract on my right eye, which now became my only hope for salvation. The medical commission examined me and decided to send me to an eye specialist to make a final determination about my category. I was the envy of my entire work brigade. Lucky stiff— confined to the hospital! I won't have to go on work detail!

That kind of good fortune doesn't come along very often in the camps.

The camp hospital was about fifty kilometers from the transit camp in Taishet. On the way there I learned what a great privilege it was to be placed on the sick list or even among those being examined for that category. You not only had to be sick, you had to be lucky too. Most prisoners who claimed illness were dismissed as fakers and malingerers. To be placed on the sick list was therefore the pinnacle of achievement. You are treated like royalty. You are not marched to your destination but are transported in the infirmary van, which has a window (barred) and is not too crowded. Those who are seriously ill even have room to lie down. True, they may be only one step away from death, but at least they are lying down.

The regimen at the hospital was much easier than at the camp. Although here too the prisoners were counted twice a day, they were not dragged out to the yard for roll call. The hospital barracks were kept cleaner for the sake of the patients, who generally were not permitted to stay there any longer than necessary.

Hospital 025 was the largest in the Taishetlag. It had twelve departments, each one handling a different set of ailments. Most of the doctors were prisoners themselves, usually specialists in their field. The ophthalmologist to whom I was assigned had been an assistant to the renowned Professor Pilatov. The chief physician, who was not a prisoner, had the final say both in establishing the final diagnosis and in determining the categories for discharged patients.

The first thing a Jewish prisoner wanted to know was whether there were other Jews in the camp. In this respect, there was nothing to complain about. Every section had its brethren in Israel. In the hospital I met Rabbi Lev of Kharkov, who had been brought in with a heart attack. (He died later in a camp.) The doctors had ordered complete bed rest for him, but the rabbi insisted, "I am among my people here," and would get up every once in a while, put on his bathrobe, and go out looking for Jews to talk with. If he came across a Jew who knew his way around the Commentaries, he wouldn't let him go. The rabbi was as full of Torah as a pomegranate is of seeds. He knew pages and pages of Talmud by heart. He too had been sentenced under article 58. Who else had more to do with the return to Zion than he did? In the eyes of Stalin's security police he was no less a counterrevolutionary than the young students who were arrested for underground Jewish nationalist activity.

I also met a number of Yiddish writers here, but I will mention only one, because he has gone to the next world and my words can do him no harm now. Hershl Kamenetsky, the Soviet Yiddish poet, a gifted lyricist and translator, was arrested with a whole group of Yiddish writers from Byelorussia. He too was lucky, in that he was tried and sentenced by a special board in Moscow and given only ten years. He had two other pieces of good luck: he had been suffering with tuberculosis for years, and the official in charge of the hospital was a Jew. This official saw no reason why the tubercular Yiddish poet who once had worked as a barber could not resume his old profession. After all, the TB patients in barracks 12 needed haircuts too.

They kept me in the eye department for seven days until Dr. T., the specialist, made his diagnosis: a cataract on the right eye, caused by a trauma. At the same time, taking into account my weakened physical condition, he assigned me to the internal medicine department, whose coordinator was a prominent Jewish doctor from Moscow.

Never shall I forget the sympathy, dedication, and brotherly concern with which this man treated me. He was in charge of two departments in the hospital, but he saw me every day and made sure I received the proper medicines. Every evening he invited me into his office, where we sat and talked for hours. It turned out that he was very much at home in both Hebrew and Yiddish literature.

The reason for his arrest was incredible. In prewar Poland the name of a certain Dr. Messing was well known among Jews. Dr. Messing was a famous hypnotist who also published books on palmistry and physiognomy. During the war, Dr. Messing fled to the Soviet Union, where he soon became known for his work in group hypnosis. My professor told me that Dr. Messing once wanted to arrange a seance in a border town but was refused permission to do so by the Soviet authorities. Dr. Messing went to see the chief of the local border police, who wondered how the doctor had got in to see him unannounced when there were several sentries outside. To which Dr. Messing replied, "Easy! I merely hypnotized them all."

Dr. T. assured me that this actually had happened and that unfortunately this ability of Dr. Messing's was later utilized by the MGB.

My professor met Dr. Messing quite by accident. An admirer of his hypnotic technique, he became friends with him to the extent of confiding his innermost thoughts to him. It therefore came as a shock to him at his trial when he was confronted with a tape recording of one of his friendly talks with Messing. The tape contained nothing counterrevolutionary, except that the professor could be heard voicing his admiration for the plucky little State of Israel. This was sufficient evidence of nationalism to get him sent away for ten years.

Barbershop attendant

I spent an entire month in the internal medicine department of the hospital and regained some of my strength. My condition was diagnosed as pellagra, or vitamin deficiency; luckily for me, such patients were given special care. This hospital was near the camp administration office and therefore was visited more frequently by commissions from Moscow. Also, the kitchen was run by a qualified dietitian and was better managed than in most other places. There was probably less stealing going on here, too. As a result of all this, the patients' meals were tastier and more nourishing.

It was a never-ending source of amazement to me that amidst this sea of cruelty, injustice, and barbarism there was still a comparatively good hospital where patients were treated conscientiously and, in many instances, even cured. It is also true that one of the slogans posted around the hospital walls was: OUR GOAL—NO PATIENT IN THE HOSPITAL LONGER THAN A MONTH!

For me too a time limit had to come, sooner or later. Dr. Nelga, the chief physician, had noted more than once in her reports that I should be discharged. The hospital administrator had received denunciations of my professor for keeping Jews in the hospital longer than regulations permitted. Nonetheless, the professor found work for me as an attendant in his own reception room and as a night watchman in the hospital barracks. Still, I remained a thorn in the side of the anti-Semites.

Dr. N., a Jewish neurologist from Vienna and chief of the psychiatric and neurological department, suggested to the professor that both of them recommend me as a helper in the camp barbershop. That way I would be able to stay there another few months before I was sent out to some remote prison camp to do hard labor. Since I had been classified as an invalid, the regulations entitled me to this kind of job.

Dr. N. was the most learned man on the hospital staff. It was a delight to listen to him talk. He was marvelously conversant with German literature, having been an habitué of the Viennese literary cafés, and had written occasional pieces himself for the *Neue Freie Presse*. He was a personal friend of Karl Kraus, the noted satirist. Dr. N. already had served two-thirds of his sentence, which began in 1937 when he was given fifteen years for spying for the Germans, even though he came to Russia from Vienna in 1933, when Hitler first took power.

Stocky, with keen, smiling eyes, his pipe perpetually in his mouth, he walked around looking for someone to kibitz with, to share a joke with. This was a much-needed relaxation for him from his work with the mentally ill, of whom there were a great number here. He was also a consultant in brain surgery. In the camp hospital Dr. N. commanded a unique kind of respect. Even the criminals, who thought nothing of beating up a doctor for not classifying them in the right category, treated Dr. N. with utmost deference. This may have been due to his sharp psychological insight and his personal approach to everyone. It was this latter quality that endeared him to the barbers in the camp.

The barbers were a privileged caste among the inmates. All the camp bigshots came to them to get their hair cut—the *naryadchik*, who supervised all the work assignments; the *kaptyorshchik*, who managed the warehouses; the chief cook; the guards and their captains; and of course the *natchalnik* himself, the chief administrator. The barbers established a scale of prices for their various services: a quick haircut and a once-over-lightly shave was one price; a customer who was treated like a free civilian with special sheets and towels was another price; face cream and powder, or even a dash of cologne, was a higher price, for the pocket of only a select few in the camp.

The manager of the barbershop was a Tatar from Odessa who looked like a Jew. He spoke a fluent Yiddish, even tossing in verses from Scriptures, which were as appropriate as dance tunes at a funeral. Crafty and cunning, he never missed an opportunity to take somebody over. Whenever he had the chief administrator under the razor he always wheedled something out of him, such as a pass to go outside the camp zone, supposedly to buy hair tonics and cologne for his shop.

He had two assistants. One was an Estonian who had owned a big farm; he got ten years for refusing to join the collective and agitating other farmers to do likewise. An easygoing sort, he did his work from eight in the morning until nine in the evening without uttering a word. The other assistant was a young Russian from the underworld who was classified as disabled because of a leg wound that refused to heal. (I later learned that it refused to heal because he kept pouring gasoline into it!)

This trio served the entire camp. Occasionally they were called upon to shave patients in the hospital prior to an operation. Because this was considered a highly desirable job, the barbers would argue over the privilege, especially if the patient was a woman. The matter usually was settled by drawing lots. The winner was sent off to work with leering requests for mementos of the occasion.

Dr. N. and my professor recommended me to the Tatar as an attendant in the barbershop, and he hired me. My duties were to sweep the floor after every haircut, shake out the sheets, wash the soap dishes, make sure there is always a supply of hot water, and keep a fire going in the stove in the cold weather. (There was plenty of kindling because I had available the shavings from the camp woodworking shop, where I made friends with a young Polish Jew.) I was also responsible for keeping the linens clean, which I did in the nearby laundry. Every day after business hours I washed the floor, polished all the mirrors, dusted the whole place, and waited for the guards to come and pick up the razors, scissors, and other deadly weapons. In short, as my boss told me, keep the whole place sparkling and don't leave a speck of dust anywhere!

Of course, I had to fetch the meals for the three barbers, but not from the regular kitchen. They made a deal with the cook to get the leftovers from the meals served to the critically ill patients, many of whom were on a more nutritious diet. In their condition the patients ate very little, so the barbers had a feast every day. After they finished their meals, I washed and dried the dishes and put them away in a special cupboard.

Most of my time was spent in the laundry, which was located near the barracks that housed the camp attendants. The manager of the laundry was a former Hero of the Soviet Union, a pilot in the air force, who had been sentenced to fifteen years for being shot down by the Germans during an air battle. His crime: he had let himself be taken alive. That later, under duress, he had signed a statement critical of the Soviet government of course prolonged the sentence. In the camp they made him manager of the laundry, a job he did in an exemplary fashion.

The pilot had a soft spot in his heart for the intelligentsia. When he learned I was a writer, he tried to make life a little easier for me. He had my wash taken care of first, and often he would bring it back to the barbershop himself. At such times he would speak to me in a friendly manner, which didn't hurt my standing with my opportunistic boss.

Even his influence wasn't enough to keep me in this sinecure permanently. I carried out my duties faithfully enough, usually returning to my barracks after the lights-out signal had sounded. Sometimes, however, I missed a cobweb or a bit of dust, mainly because of the injury to my right eye that I sustained in a Siberian labor battalion during the war. Dr. Nelga, a dark-eyed Tatar beauty, used to visit the shop frequently to get her eyebrows done. For some reason, whenever she came in, she would run her delicate fingers over the mirrors or the windows and come up gloatingly with a smudge. I had friends among the doctors who defended me sympathetically and requested that I be left where I was at least until the worst frosts were over. My boss cautioned me, "Dust—that's your main enemy. Over a speck of the stuff you'll have to leave this place sooner or later!"

In his crafty eyes I discerned what he was really after. He wanted my one good suit, which the thieves on the train had left me out of all my belongings for being a good boy. It was this suit of imported cloth that he had offered to swap me long ago for his cheap suit of black linen, which could be bought in the camp anyway. My suit was very precious to me; it was the last and final reminder of life in freedom. Furthermore, I simply didn't feel like knuckling under to the brazen cupidity of this operator, who wasn't satisfied no matter how much he had and who wanted to own whatever he laid eyes on. So I didn't attempt to bribe him.

It didn't take long for him to get back at me. About a month later I suddenly was ordered to report to the convoy guard. My new destination was not very far away. The Jewish doctors had got that much out of the *naryadchik* at least. My new home was sector 021, only five kilometers from the hospital, but the prisoners had to get there on foot.

Ben Slutsky

At this point I interrupt the narrative to tell about one of my fellow inmates who had served time with the murdered Soviet Yiddish writers while they were in the Butyrki and Lubyanka prisons in Moscow. Ben Slutsky—who for some reason escaped their fate—settled in Birobidzhan after the war and was arrested there at the same time I was. He died in prison before the day of liberation arrived.

Before the war Ben Slutsky was known widely for his lexicographical work and his Yiddish translations of Russian literary classics. His translation of Tolstoy's *Anna Karenina* was published by the Kiev Publishing House of National Minorities in the 1930s. He also wrote a few short stories. At the time of his arrest Slutsky was working on a long historical novel about the Bar Kochba period in Jewish history. He had completed several sections of the book and had read them to Yiddish writers in Birobidzhan.

Slutsky looked older than his seventy years. His wife died during the evacuation to the East, leaving him with a young daughter from her first husband. In Birobidzhan, Slutsky was put in charge of the Jewish section of the regional geographical museum, a task to which he gave his heart and soul and much self-sacrificing work. Old and frail, he was nevertheless indefatigable. He gathered together a great treasury of rare collections and memorabilia that illustrate the path of the Jews through history; he did not omit items having to do with Jewish religious life, keeping in mind especially younger audiences, who no longer had any visual concepts about that part of their history to relate to.

It was for that very reason that the gray-haired scholar had to face judicial charges. In the factual evidence (which filled several volumes of the investigative record of our case) we saw clippings from the *Jewish Daily Forward* of New York going back to the 1920s. In those days Ben Slutsky was the Kiev correspondent of the *Forward*, signing himself "Kievski." This evidence consisted of dispatches he had written describing the productivization of former Jewish petty traders in Russia. In the indictment this was called *kleveta*— slander; Slutsky, in his dispatches, was slandering and defaming the good name of the USSR abroad. In a word, the old man was labeled not only a Jewish nationalist but a scandal-monger.

One of the witnesses against Slutsky was another Yiddish writer who later was executed. Evidently, under torture, he testified that Slutsky had sent materials to the Jewish Anti-Fascist Committee in Moscow concerning Jewish evacuees in Kazakhstan, including a description of military installations where the Jewish evacuees were working. Of course, Slutsky had done this deliberately, knowing that these stories would be sent to publications abroad by the witness, who worked on the Jewish Anti-Fascist Committee.

INTERROGATOR: Why did the witness want to send these materials abroad?

The answer of the tortured Yiddish writer was that for years he had been working for a foreign espionage service. (There wasn't one Yiddish writer about whom this witness was not questioned.) The same witness had a most phenomenal memory. He testified that he had met me through the writer Leo Finkelstein, who introduced us in Bialystok in 1940. He also stated that all my dispatches were written in a "nationalist spirit" and that I was an intimate friend of the "leader of the Jewish nationalists," Solomon Mikhoels. I'm sure God has forgiven that poor, unfortunate man. His interrogators must have tormented him beyond endurance.

Later I learned another interesting fact from a man who had served his sentence with a former Soviet general, the husband of the famous Russian singer Ruslanova. The general shared a cell with the above-mentioned Yiddish writer in a Moscow jail. It seems that the Yiddish poet became very pious in prison and would not even tear a piece of paper on the Sabbath. The general gladly acted as his Shabbes goy.

Ben Slutsky received a harsher sentence than the rest of us. His term was ten years in prison, not a forced labor camp. It is true that in prison you are not forced to work like a slave, but in a labor camp you are usually out in the open air, living and working with other human beings. Slutsky was sent to the infamous Alexandrovka, an old prison sixty kilometers from Irkutsk situated among high cliffs. The prisoner is buried alive, cut off from the rest of the world.

The last time I saw Slutsky we were in a Stolypin car being transported from the investigatory prison to our incarceration points. Slutsky knew where they were taking him, but he was so exhausted from the interrogation that he was completely indifferent to everything around him. He could not stop weeping and lamenting the fate of his wife's young daughter, who was being left all alone in the world. He was a broken man; there was no resistance left in him. In 1956 I received the sad news from his stepdaughter. He had died in 1954, two years before our release and "rehabilitation."

Penal servitude

To get from the hospital to the invalids' camp is a long, four-hour march over a road that leads up steep hills and down deep valleys piled high with snow. It is early October. The temperature is 15 below, but the sun on the snow is blinding. The hills around us are blanketed with thick forest, the trees so laden with snow that the bent branches almost touch the ground. Amidst the trees—such stillness, such dreaminess! Even our footsteps—the tread of a hundred and fifty slaves—make no sound. For a while I forget that I am being dragged along here by a dozen armed guards and as many vicious dogs.

I am a prisoner, but how delighted my eyes are as they fly like free birds over the entire horizon, reveling in the beauty of God's creation. You forget for a moment that you are a bird in a cage, but only for a moment. Then your eyes pick up the cruel expressions of the convoy guards, their brutality to the unfortunate cripples who must climb the hills on their crutches and keep sliding back in the snow. Many of these cripples only recently have had a leg amputated as a result of frostbite brought on by working outdoors or standing in line for hours at repeated roll calls. The invalids keep stumbling like helpless infants learning to walk, but the guards curse at them to keep moving and beat them for falling behind.

Your feet sink so deep into the snow you can't pull them out. Prisoners toss away their pitiful bundles of belongings, which are slowing them down. The groaning of the amputees assails the ears, as does the nerve-shattering barking of the police dogs. Long before you reach your destination you are bone weary and dispirited.

Fifty yards from the camp the overseers already are waiting for us. At once they begin the ritual of calling out the names of the prisoners. Each man must answer with his year of birth and the number of the article under which he was sentenced. This procedure takes several hours. Not until it is finished does the warden begin his inspection of the new arrivals.

We are lined up across a big open field, people of various races and colors, a real internationale—Kirghizes, Tatars, Uzbeks, Ukrainians, Russians, Mongols, Bashkiri, Jews, and I, the ex-yeshiva student. Grishko the warden and his aides walk around, studying the new merchandise. They look into our mouths, feel our muscles, and tap our backs, exactly like peasants examining horses at a fair in my hometown of Ostrów Mazowiecka. All at once Grishko roars, "This lousy junk is not for me! Have they nothing better to do than send me their shit?"

True, camp 021 was an invalids' camp and therefore was not given any important projects. But it did have a central tailoring and shoe-repair shop. This work could be done sitting down, they could employ people without legs, the old and the sick; our shipment must have looked practically senile, however, especially since the clothes they had given us to wear were suitable only for human castoffs—tattered, stained, and full of patches. Even the shoes we wore were not paired. The amputees among us leaned on their crutches or simply stretched out in the wet snow. Every few moments another one of them took sick or passed out, and a doctor had to be summoned. Most of these people were heart cases or recovering from jaundice, which was quite prevalent in the camps.

In a word, the warden had cause to be miffed at the

camp administration for sending him a shipment of such poor quality. Telephones started ringing. Grishko wanted to return the whole lot as inferior goods, decidedly not what he had ordered. The administration, however, objected that there was nowhere else to send us. The merchandise, in the meantime, stood in the freezing cold, outside the camp gate, waiting for the bosses to straighten out their differences and let us in.

The place where I was sent to spend my next ten years consisted of eight larger barracks for the prisoners and a couple of smaller buildings for the administration offices and services. In the latter were a kitchen, a canteen, a bathhouse, and a special room for the bigshots who came to visit the camp or acquaint themselves with the work done here. Also the Department of Culture and Education, whose real function was to spy on the prisoners, but definitely not to "re-educate them in the Soviet spirit." For the record, there was also a small library here.

In the work area were a large barracks for the tailoring and shoe-repair shop, a small electric generator, and a carpentry shop; also piles of logs, which the prisoners sawed into boards for repairing the rotting structures or for fuel.

When we arrived, the camp had just completed its chore known as *shporka klapov*—killing the bedbugs with boiling water. The makeshift bunks were carried outside, and the invalids (who were supposed to work indoors) were busy all day at this disgusting work. This procedure was repeated every few months. Huge tubs are placed outside and filled with boiling water. The bunks are taken apart and the boards dunked into the boiling water to drive out the armies of bugs that lie in wait for the cold and exhausted inmates dying for sleep after a day at hard labor. For a month after the bunks are scoured, and the straw mattresses frozen in the subzero air, and the walls of the barracks whitewashed, we are rid of these loathsome pests. And then they gradually return.

The process of *shporka klapov*, however, is not exactly salutary for the inmates while it is taking place. Until the work is finished they must stand around outside in the cold and the snow. For us newcomers it was even worse. We had just marched for half a day, and there was nowhere to warm up or rest our bones. Luckily, we were taken into the canteen for a little while, where it was warm and where they gave us some hot food to revive us. It was here that we Jewish prisoners immediately sensed the warmth and friendliness of the Jewish tailors and shoemakers who had been in the camp a long time, some since 1940—Jews from Poland, Bessarabia, the Ukraine, imprisoned here under a variety of charges. They received us as brothers.

I want to mention especially Isaac Weiner, a young man from Rovno, who eventually made his way to Israel. Weiner was a wonderfully sensitive person with a big heart. Strong and handsome, he made friends with all the prisoners who had managed to establish themselves in some kind of official position, such as the managers of the food and clothing warehouses or the head of the *chleborezka*, where the daily bread ration was sliced and weighed. His connections with these people helped him to get extra bread for new Jewish prisoners.

The tailors' barracks was privileged. In general, tailoring was a highly esteemed trade in the camps. The tailors were not guarded as closely, and their regimen was easier. They were even permitted to hang pictures on their walls. Each tailor made his own little corner as comfortable and as pleasant as he could. The tailors did not have to shave their heads. Some of them wore their own clothes, which under the circumstances made them look positively elegant. Who were they dressing up for? For the pretty, dark-eyed Jewish woman who had the exalted position of controller in the camp workshops. She was the only woman around, and as soon as she appeared anywhere hundreds of eyes went through her like spears.

When Isaac Weiner escaped from the German occupation in Rovno, he was still a boy. His adventures in the Soviet Union would read like an Arabian Nights' tale. Suffice it to say that eventually he was sentenced to death, but because of his youth the term was commuted to ten years at hard labor. In one of the camps, where he had been working in the lime pits, a Nazi prisoner called him "Jew bastard" and a few other choice compliments. In a blind rage, Weiner picked up the Nazi and threw him into the lime oven. For this he was given an additional sentence. A proud Jew, he never hesitated to challenge anyone who ran off at the mouth with Jew-baiting remarks.

Later, when I also had become an old settler, Weiner and I began to compile lists of all the Jews in the camp. Whenever a new convoy arrived, he would manage to find extra bread rations for his starving brothers.

For people who live in freedom—especially in a rich country like the United States—it may sound ludicrous to make such a fuss over an extra slice of bread. But in the camps where we served our tenners there wasn't very much else to eat. We got—or were supposed to get—two grams of fat a day. Meat we never saw at all. The fish they gave us was so rotten or salty that it took an effort to put it into our mouths. Aside from the bit of oatmeal, bread was the only food we got that was filling and nourishing. So Isaac Weiner saved many of us from starvation and possibly death in those grim days.

Gradually I grew accustomed to the new place and the new life. I was assigned an upper bunk in a corner. Weiner matched me up with a good brigade leader, Pyotr Krushkin, a man past sixty but still strong and agile. Kushkin had been director of a factory. In 1937 he was arrested for *boltavnya* —loose talk—and sent up for ten years. Since he blabbed only because he'd had a few drinks too many, his sentence was reduced to five years. In 1941 he was released and sent back to his factory, which was now manufacturing weapons.

Krushkin was a capable manager and an excellent organizer; he kept his factory running smoothly and efficiently.

But his old thirst for the hard stuff had grown even more acute during his years in the prison camp. When he returned to freedom he couldn't resist indulging himself once in a while. One day an old friend of his, an army colonel, before going off to the front, invited him to his home for his wife's birthday party. With a few vodkas under their belts, they got to talking high politics. Evidently Krushkin offered his opinion that if Stalin hadn't signed the friendship pact with Hitler the war might have been avoided. This so shocked the colonel that he exploded. "You're nothing but an enemy of the people, Krushkin! No wonder they sent you up in '37!" Unfortunately, Krushkin was carrying a revolver. He shot his friend in the head.

The penalty for killing an officer in wartime is death. But again Krushkin was lucky. The court took into account the fact that the colonel had grievously insulted him and that after the fifth drink it was not easy for Krushkin to control his indignation. He got away with a fresh tenner under article 59, which classified his crime as ordinary banditry without any political intent whatsoever.

Professor S.

Pyotr Krushkin would become very agitated when he led his brigade of invalids out to work. He would swear and curse at us with every variety of "mother" oath known to man, but by nature he wasn't really so bad. Many times he would look the other way when we weren't doing our work according to regulations.

As invalids they gave us work inside the camp zone. Every day we had to bring the water for the bathhouse, for the kitchen, for tea for all the barracks. This water had to be carried in buckets from a stream. We shoveled the snow off the camp grounds, we cleared the ice out of the stream, we kept the barracks supplied with firewood, we helped wash the floors. We peeled potatoes in the kitchen—when they were lucky enough to have them. We lugged the food from the warehouse to the kitchen. And we did all the other chores relating to the service of the camp.

Krushkin thought most highly of those individuals who did whatever they were told without making a fuss about it. For that reason he rewarded me with a wonderful bunk neighbor, the grizzly Professor S. Seventy years old, with the constitution of a man half his age, Professor S. would do his sit-ups every morning in the open air, half-undressed even in the coldest weather. His muscles were hard, his body well toned. From our very first conversation I trusted him implicitly. His knowledge was immense and his personal traits most rare.

He was a Finn by nationality. Born in a village near Helsinki, his well-to-do father had provided him with a superb education. He was graduated from the University of St. Petersburg with honors and became a doctoral student just prior to World War I. Still quite young when he received his Ph.D., he went to the Sorbonne to continue his studies. Later he settled in Lithuania, where he taught at the University of Kovno, pursued his research, and published textbooks in the Lithuanian language. The Lithuanian government had so much faith in him that they entrusted him with a diplomatic pouch on his frequent trips to Paris. This proved his undoing. The MGB charged him with open espionage and sentenced him under article 58, section 6.

For whom had this honorable, sensitive professor spied? Nobody. He had to wait until after Stalin's death, when the charge was nullified and the professor was "rehabilitated." In the meantime, this fine scholar and humanist was sentenced to fifteen years in a prison camp. Krushkin used to joke with him about his long sentence. "Comrade Professor, you'll have to borrow a few years from the prosecutor if he expects you to serve out the whole fifteen years."

Professor S., who had mastered six European languages and was well versed also in logic and philosophy, was my partner in our camp duties. For years we did the hard, dirty labor together; together we were transferred from camp to camp; and together we felt the lash of the assorted scoundrels, bosses, and brigadiers. This elderly professor never once asked for easier work. If I ever stopped him from lifting a heavy log, he became indignant. Although he was physically strong, his legs often swelled up; after a couple of days' rest in his bunk the swelling would go down and he again would be ready for the heaviest kind of work, as though he were doing penance. It was a pleasure to work with him. He knew many scholarly works by heart and was always glad to share his knowledge with a fellow prisoner.

Years later, after the bloody uprisings in the camps at

Vorkuta, Norilsk, Kolyma, Fergana, and some parts of the Taishetlag—when the Beria terror began to relax, when the Central Committee of the Communist Party called special meetings and sent commissions into the camps to study the situation on the spot—Professor S. was permitted to lecture to the prisoners on scientific matters and to answer questions at the block meetings. His fiery arguments with anti-Semites were memorable experiences.

In 1955, when prisoners were allowed to receive books from home, the library in Professor S.'s corner of the barracks quickly filled up with volumes in various languages. One day he radiantly handed me a Russian edition of the letters of Pliny the Younger. Pliny, governor of Sicily, writing to Emperor Hadrian about the Christian sects who refused to worship the Roman gods, informs the emperor that during religious ceremonies these strange people eat only their own "pure bread." At the end of the book there is an explanation of the phrase "pure bread" and a note to the effect that the Christians are suspected of kneading the blood of Roman children into it.

"You see," the old professor declared triumphantly, "the blood libel has a long and dishonorable history!"

He carried this book around with him and fearlessly showed it to all the anti-Semites in the camp. "Look, your fairy tale about Jews using Christian blood to make matzo was invented by the ancient Romans to make trouble for the first Christians!"

That's why it was a pleasure for me to work with the professor, to chop wood with him, to carry it around to all the barracks, to haul water from the stream winter and summer, bucket after bucket, with one end of the pole on my shoulder and the other end on his, enough water to satisfy the daily need of eight hundred hungry and thirsty prisoners.

How to handle a Jew-baiter

Our brigade had a high proportion of people from the intelligentsia. There was, for example, Constantin Shakanis, minister of education in the Lithuanian government, who had translated Adam Mickiewicz's classic poem *Pan Tadeusz* from the Polish. Shakanis was arrested a month after the Russians occupied his country. Already in his late seventies, this venerable man died in the prison camp.

Then there was an Estonian lawyer who, as a result of high blood pressure and a dozen other ailments, had become mentally unbalanced. His sister was selling off her personal jewelry (which she had managed to hide) so she could send him food parcels twice a month. With these packages he was bribing the work assigners to exempt him from the daily regimen. An inveterate anti-Semite, this lawyer became friendly with the Nazi doctor Moesbach, who had more than one Jewish death on his conscience.

At that time we still knew very little of the doctor's Nazi background. We knew even less about the role Nazi physicians played in the destruction of European Jewry. Some of the German prisoners in the camp tried to act correctly and even friendly toward the Jewish prisoners, but Moesbach couldn't even look a Jew in the eye. When he was assigned to work in the camp hospital, he openly baited the Jewish patients. It was easy to imagine what this loathsome creature had done to Jews when he had the power during the Nazi "night of the long knife."

These two anti-Semites—the German doctor and the Estonian lawyer—would conduct their Jew-hating conversations at a decibel level that could be heard by everyone around them. In our brigade there were only two or three Jews besides me. One of them, a very sick man, had been sent up in 1937 for owning a copy of Bukharin's *ABCs of Communism* (a book that had been published in many editions by the Soviet State Publishing House until its author became a "traitor"). I don't think there was an organ in this man's body that wasn't diseased or malfunctioning. During the first year of the war, the camp he was in was evacuated overnight and moved to another location. That night many of the prisoners were shot. Although he was one of the lucky ones to be spared, his hair turned completely white. Barely forty years old, he looked sixty. A religious man, his parched blue lips were constantly whispering something, as if in prayer. The only camp food he ate was his daily ration of bread and a spoonful of sugar.

Compared to him, the second Jew in our squad was a giant. The only reason he was in the invalid brigade was that all the fingers of his right hand had been severed in an accident with the camp's electric saw. He was still able to perform wonders with the fingers of his left hand. Working as a porter in the flour mill, he loaded trucks all day with his one hand, lifting the heavy sacks and tossing them to the man above him. By trade a butcher from Moscow, he was serving time because of Golda—he had been among the hundreds of Jews arrested for openly expressing enthusiasm for Golda Meir, first ambassador from the State of Israel. No one who insulted him got away with it. Many an anti-Semitic hooligan in the camp felt the butcher's left fist on his jaw. "Shut your dirty mouth, you louse, or I'll knock your teeth down your throat!" There was no doubt in his voice that he could do it.

Professor S. and I once were reprimanding the lawyer and the doctor for baiting the sick Jew in our squad and calling him faker. The butcher from Moscow, who happened by, asked me to warn these Nazi hooligans in their own language that one night he would strangle them both if they didn't keep their traps shut. In transmitting his message I was slightly less violent in my language and said that if they didn't stop their anti-Semitic slurs "this gentlemen intends to squeeze your windpipes" with his one good hand.

The butcher interrupted me brusquely. "Squeeze, shmeeze! Tell them straight out in plain language. I'll strangle those snakes and put them both out of business!"

This time I gave them the message verbatim. It worked for a while; we didn't hear a peep out of them. Later, when they started up again, the butcher tried another method: he declared a strike. He refused to load any more sacks until both those loudmouths went to work like everybody else in the brigade. Where did they get off calling other people fakers when they were the biggest phonies in the camp! Let the *natchalnik* bring in a doctor to examine them and see if they aren't a hundred times healthier than that old man who can't even get excused from work.

The warehouse loading platform kept piling up. Although Krushkin, our brigade leader, was one of the beneficiaries of the lawyer's food packages, he just naturally hated these two malingerers and resented the idea of defending them against the honest workers in his brigade. Having no alternative, he sent them both out to chop the ice in the stream. This method proved even more effective than the threat to strangle them in their sleep. Every day they came back from their labors gasping and groaning and so tired that they had no taste for their favorite pastime of baiting Jews.

Also in our brigade were the two Stoma brothers, a well-known pair of Soviet inventors. *Samorodkas*—men with natural, innate abilities, without benefit of a higher education—they had succeeded in producing a number of important inventions. One of these was in use on the Moscow subway, a device that could stop a train in an emergency. The elder Stoma, a bachelor with a white beard, kept writing reports and complaints about royalties due him on his patents.

"What would you do with all that money anyway?" Krushkin used to kid him. "The *natchalnik* would only take it away from you. You're better off leaving it to your sister."

In the same way that Stoma fought for his money, another member of our brigade, an engineer named Kuznetsov, fought against his imprisonment for diversionary activity and sabotage. As an engineer he had worked up a model for a boiler. The authorities invested several million rubles to manufacture it, only to discover that there was a flaw in the model. The engineer was charged with sabotage for the enemy.

"Just because I made one mistake," he kept insisting, "does that mean I'm an enemy? I was only trying to help the government."

Kuznetsov was a man of many talents—a fine painter, a good sculptor, a man with golden hands. He and Stoma tried to convince the camp administration to open a projects office in the camp. They drew up plans for a camp factory to produce starch from potato peelings or absorbent cotton from discarded rags. In whatever camp they were serving time, they tried in this way to get out of the hard labor regimen. They would spend months in an office on their projects until a notice came down from above that their whole plan was impossible or that it had already been done a long time ago without any help from them. Once again the inventors would have to leave their office and return to their general duties in the camp.

I become one of the gang

One day we were ordered to go pick up numbers and sew them onto every piece of our clothing. This number, corresponding with the number of our particular case, henceforth must appear on our jackets and overcoats on a patch. The prisoners raised objections. What a disgrace! When Hitler did that to the Jews, at least it was in line with his murderous anti-Semitic program; he was a cutthroat who never preached about a just world. But only two years earlier, the Soviet government had produced a film entitled "Human Being Number 217," about the Nazi degradation of human beings who no longer had a name, only a number. Now they were doing the same thing to us!

"These numbers," we were told, "must be picked up today, Sunday, without fail, and must be kept clean and legible at all times. Violators of this regulation will be punished!"

The prisoners finally agreed. "Let's take the goddamn numbers! If anybody's got to be ashamed about it, let it be *them* for making us wear such things!"

My number was Y-265.

Looking back after all these years at the incident I'm about to relate, I still wonder where I got the courage to do it. Perhaps I had become hardened in the contests with my interrogators, who tried so hard to prove my involvement in the most heinous crimes. The hatred and contempt I came to feel for all these functionaries—who knew that their accusations were false yet kept torturing me physically and mentally—only strengthened my will, my courage, and my endurance and made it possible for me to do something so contrary to my nature.

We were working on one of the usual projects of camp 051—digging a ditch for a pipe to carry water two miles to a railroad station. The work had been started by other prisoners before us but had been halted temporarily. In the meantime the ditch had filled up with water and frozen over. Marching to and from work was enough to sap your strength and freeze your bones. The three-mile hike from the camp to the work site did not go straight across fields; the convoy tried to avoid the farmhouses in the area lest we establish contact with the local population. We marched across terrain that lay under three feet of snow. We zigzagged through the woods. We crossed a stream on a makeshift bridge of loose boards, which rocked and swayed beneath our feet. Then we climbed up an embankment to the railroad tracks.

The work was punishing. The frozen ground was like rock. We chopped at it with heavy pickaxes and thirty-pound sledgehammers. The quota for ten hours of work was one cubic meter of earth. The 750 grams of bread and the bowl of gruel that were our daily fare were not enough to replenish our strength. Out in the fresh, frosty air, amid field and forest, the appetite was insatiable. The ration of bread for the long workday was swallowed in one gulp, and when we got back to the barracks there was nothing more to quiet our hunger.

And that quota! You chop and chop away at the rock and barely break off a few crumbs of dirt. I watched the strong, young Ukrainians; they too were laboring mightily, but by the end of the day they usually had made their norm. I tried to figure out the secret of wielding that pickaxe—brains evidently had very little to do with it. I was prepared to match my brains with the other prisoners, but where would I get the brawn? And the foremen didn't play games. If you didn't make your quota—*shtrafnoy payok*—they cut your ration: no more than 400 grams of bread a day and maybe a mouthful of watery soup, and you still had to make your norm. I learned to dig soft earth at the rate of four cubic meters a day, but I couldn't manage to overcome that rocky, frozen soil.

Our squad leader for this particular job happened to be a criminal of the first order, a big Ukrainian who always padded the work record of his friends and buddies. After several days of unfulfilled norms, he assigned me to chopping ice out of the ditch, a job at which I'd have a better chance of meeting the quota. At this work you needed to warm yourself once in a while. Standing all day long with your boots immersed in ice-cold water, your feet froze to the rubber and slowed down the circulation of the blood. My brigadier, however, didn't allow me any time by the fire. My feet froze and my body steamed. I took off my padded jacket and worked in my shirtsleeves. According to all the laws of physiology (especially in my weakened condition), I should have come down with pneumonia or at least a high fever. Nothing like that happened. When I finally dragged myself back to the barracks that evening I went straight to the dispensary for an examination, hoping the thermometer would show the lucky 37.6 degrees centigrade so I could get a respite from the frozen ditch for a day or two.

Apparently the human body accommodates itself to everything. Even tuberculosis patients were cured in this camp—a cure I wish on all my enemies. For some reason the lesions on their lungs healed and they stopped spitting up blood. The foremen drove these unfortunate devils all the harder.

In a prison camp no complaints are accepted. On the contrary, they are usually met with well-placed punches to the ribs, where they won't show. The brigadier is boss. His sole responsibility is to keep you working on the job; it is his privilege to evaluate the worth of each prisoner entrusted to him. On the dossier that accompanies the offender from prison to camp is a record of his conduct. This information is provided by the brigade leader. It is enough for him to look at you cross-eyed, and your record will contain so many negative characteristics that even after you serve your full sentence you'll never see the light of day again or be eligible for the rare amnesty proclaimed on special national observances.

No matter how often I begged him, my squad leader refused to let me stand by the fire, even for a few minutes. One afternoon a wild, extraordinary idea gradually matured in my head. I picked up a heavy branch from the ground, walked straight up to him, and hit him over the head!

Me and my brigadier—David and Goliath! If he had hit me with that same stick I never would have lived to tell the story. He merely dropped to his knees momentarily, blood gushing from a cut in his head. All the escort guards came running. They roughed me up, handcuffed me, and threw me in the hole, where I stayed for ten days and nights.

Was I a hero? I believe it was more an expression of despair than of conscious protest. It was a consequence of the pain accumulated over the years. Perhaps it was also an attempt at suicide, which I hadn't the nerve to commit in any other way. As I felt his head give way beneath the stick, I was certain my own life was finished. Whatever the reason, the fact remains I did it.

At the end of my period of incarceration they sent me back to work with the same squad leader, who had recovered sooner than I did. I bid a last farewell to my friends and gave them the addresses of people who should be notified of my demise. Sending me back to work under that leader was tantamount to a death sentence.

He was still wearing a bandage around his head. I reported for work and waited for my execution. Not that it necessarily would be carried out by him. He had plenty of assistants who were ready and able to do the job as well as he could.

To my astonishment he only stuck out his hand and said with a big smile, "*Ti chevo nye skazal?* Hey, why didn't you tell us before? (Meaning, if you're not afraid to crack somebody's head open, you must be one of us, so why have you kept it a secret?) *Skazhi, ti kavo nibud ubil?* Tell me, did you ever finish anybody off?"

"*Koneshno! Imeyu pyat chelovek na shchetu!* Certainly. My score is five!" I said, without batting an eye.

And that's how I became one of the gang, a guy who could dish out a punch when necessary and to hell with the consequences. My squad leader now sent me over to the fire at every opportunity. Who needs writers, poets, people of culture? Give them a taste of your fist, then they become your pals.

From that day on, I passed as a criminal offender, playing the role so well that I kept a tough look on my face even in my sleep. My Jewish friends in the brigade were careful not to give me away. Quite the opposite. They tried to augment my credentials with the brigadier, feeding him one tale after another about my life of crime. They too benefited from my new status.

Moishe Broderson

I had been in the Taishet camp for many months. I had become an old-timer, had grown accustomed to the dangers that lay in wait for the inmates and learned how to guard against them. I knew exactly what kind of work I was suited best for. I had learned how to mix clay, lime, and cement; how to dig ditches; how to plaster a wall; how to carry bricks up ladders in a hod and to crawl through attics with them. I had made friends, Jews and non-Jews. Daytime we worked long and hard; evenings we got together and reminisced about our life in freedom—was it gone forever?

The time began to drag. One evening a transport of new prisoners arrived at the camp. When the train pulled in, all of us—after a long day's labor—ran to the barracks of the immigrants, eager to learn if there was an old friend or acquaintance among them.

My feelings when I first caught sight of Moishe Broderson are indescribable. How happy I was to see him! How wretched he looked! I remember he was still wearing his brown felt hat. (A hat was a rarity in the camps, for we were given a regulation cap. Later the amateur dramatic group used Broderson's hat as a prop.) He had on a padded overcoat with a wide, fur collar. A battered old knapsack hung over his shoulder. Of his one-time elegance only his remarkable eyes remained, but now they were veiled with a film of fear. They seemed somehow larger, shocked by what they saw.

Broderson last had been in camp 045 near Bratsk, where after many efforts had been made on his behalf he was assigned to the relatively easy job of bathhouse attendant. With water so scarce there (it had to be transported a distance), his job was to regulate the amount put in the buckets. The criminals in the camp had made his life miserable, robbing him of the packages sent to him by his wife, Sheyne Miriam.

When he saw me he fell on my shoulders and burst into tears. For a long while he could not utter a word, only looking at me silently and weeping spasmodically. When he finally got control of himself he began to stammer, as people do when they have so much to tell they don't know where to start. He had not been arrested until 1950, later than I and later than many of the other Yiddish writers in Moscow. Until the moment they came for him, every day was filled with terror. Now this once irrepressible man I had known in Poland stood before me bent over and sad-eyed, clutching his heart.

"That we should have lived to see this!" he sobbed. In that single phrase he told his whole story.

I immediately went and found Isaac Weiner, the young man who took care of all the new Jewish arrivals. The first thing he had to do was put a stop to the bullying that Broderson was being subjected to by the gang of thieves in his transport. That didn't take long. Isaac soon made it clear to them that in this camp they wouldn't get away with the kind of abuse they had perpetrated in 045.

As a result, Moishe Broderson gradually regained his composure. He made the acquaintance of our good Dr. S., who ordered Broderson's squad leader to excuse him from hard labor for the time being. Broderson was given the duties of night watchman, a job he held as long as he was in that camp. He was required to do five hours of guard duty a night to prevent fire and thievery. He also was responsible for getting all the prisoners to line up for evening roll call.

Because he was supposed to prevent smoking inside the barracks, he had to stay awake at night. With his inborn good nature and his unfailing sense of humor, he was not very strict about this either with himself or with others, a weakness for which he frequently paid with time in the guardhouse. The camp watchman, sneaking into the barracks and finding him dozing over a book, would pour cold water down his collar. Broderson didn't like this, of course, but what bothered him even more was carrying out the latrine buckets with all the bodily waste of the night.

In general, Broderson looked like a little, harmless bird that accidentally had wandered into the camp. The numbers on his back and his trousers seemed completely out of place on him. Before long he was making jokes about the whole absurd game.

The war in Korea had begun; the bloodshed there foretold a world conflagration. Moscow *Pravda* was full of daily greetings to Stalin on his seventieth birthday. The newspaper had two columns headed POTOK PRIVYETSVIYE— Stream of Greetings—as if nothing else were going on in the world. All year long the stream of congratulations flowed unceasingly, except for one editorial, in the most crucial days of the war, stressing the need to strengthen the science of astronomy!

"You know what it reminds me of?" said Broderson to me one morning, pointing to the men lined up for roll call. "The same kind of game is being played here. A man will smack the person in front of him on the back, and when the other guy turns around, all he sees is a man looking up innocently at the sky. Those people in Moscow are doing the same thing—looking up at the sky. They had nothing to do with it."

The rumor that our camp was being moved two hundred kilometers farther east proved to be true. Our brigade was assigned to move all the machines into the freight cars, a project we worked on twenty-four hours at a stretch. We also had to empty the storehouses and load the material into the cars.

The prisoners were divided into two groups of five hundred to be transported to the new camp. It was a hot day in June when we lined up for the big move. Broderson and I landed in the first group. The trip took three days and three nights, and we were locked in those hot, airless cars the whole time. The strongest prisoners took over the lower bunks, where the air was a little cooler. Broderson and I were pushed up to the top bunks. During that entire three-day period he didn't eat a thing. Several times he passed out. We persuaded the guards to move him to the infirmary car, but they didn't let him stay there long—he had no temperature. Fainting and weakness without a temperature are not considered an illness in Soviet prison camps.

Captain Yermilov, the chief of our new camp 051, approached the job entrusted to him with utmost efficiency. Some twelve hundred of us had been sent to a site that had been neglected almost to the point of abandonment. After the Japanese war prisoners who had built it were released, the camp had been inhabited by offenders who were permitted to live only in a prescribed region. Outside of their inheritance in the whiskey cellars, the new inmates didn't take care of anything in the camp. The free citizens in the nearby villages had liberated from the barracks a mass of boards, bricks, windowpanes, and the like, which were in great demand in that area.

When we arrived we found a ruin. The narrow footpaths leading from barrack to barrack were covered with rubble, garbage, and human waste. Lumber lay all over the work areas. The tool sheds had collapsed. The furniture in the canteen and the kitchen had been cleaned out.

Yermilov lined us up the same day and issued a decree: "You have two months to turn this place into the best camp in the Taishetlag!"

There was supposed to be a central tailoring shop and a furniture factory in our camp to serve the whole Taishet-lag. In addition, Yermilov made an agreement with the railroad to lay three kilometers of water pipes underground. We had to chop down the trees around the camp and cut up the lumber—another good source of income for Yermilov. And, of course, we had to take care of all the needs of the prisoners themselves.

For two months we slept on the bare floors of the barracks and ate our meals off the floor of the mess hall. But what miracles we accomplished in that time! We had arrived at the end of June. By early August our camp positively sparkled. The entire area was cleaned, and the barracks were rebuilt from the ground up.

Yermilov recognized no dead weight, that is, a prisoner who did not work. Strong men like me toted logs, dragged lumber, sawed tree trunks, and helped the master builders. Weaker men carted away the rubble and the dirt, cleaned up, and mixed and delivered the clay and the mortar. Men without legs were organized into squads to make nails out of heavy wire. One Yiddish writer became an expert log-sawer—the cleanest and easiest work in the camp. Moishe Broderson was put in a general construction squad, pouring and mixing lime and handing it to the painters on the ladders. For Yermilov, sick people simply did not exist. The infirmary temporarily was shut down. Our doctor, a Ukrainian prisoner, whom we later found to be a selfless friend of the inmates, was forced to do the most menial work during those two months. As Yermilov explained, "You will all rest later. Now everybody works! So long as the camp is not rebuilt, I don't recognize any illnesses. Forget about your rheumatism, your bellyaches, your weak hearts, and all the other tricks you use to get out of doing honest work."

Gradually we grew accustomed to Yermilov's cruelty and caprices. The various nationalities in the camp slowly emerged, with all their faults and virtues. Unfamiliar faces grew familiar as we worked together, marched together in all kinds of weather, and listened together to the deadly threats of the convoy guards. In ranks of four and five we marched arm in arm, holding up those who were in danger of faltering or dropping to the ground, which could mean instant death. Together we huddled around the fire in the bitter cold, sharing our hand-rolled cigarettes; together we protested inwardly the coarse insults of a brutal guard or a boorish brigadier.

In the summer days—which all the world enjoys so much—when we were tortured by the millions of mosquitoes that refused to retreat even when we were wearing netting, we once more saw evidence of the deep humanity that lay right under the thick skin of the prisoners. How often it happened that a man would take off his mosquito netting and give it to someone whose netting had torn! The benefactor then would smear his own face with axle grease, whose odor repels mosquitoes.

Slowly our life fell into a routine. We began to recognize each other. We learned whom to trust and whom to avoid. Evenings we would sneak into another barracks (although that was against regulations) and talk with other Jews. There were Jews from Moscow who had been arrested because of Golda; Jews arrested over the Birobidzhan affair; Yiddish writers charged with nationalism; assimilated Jews; and old Jewish Communist Party workers who had been accused of Trotskyism, thrown into jail, later freed, and now rearrested for their old sins.

We had a little colony of Yiddish writers and Russian Jewish journalists, including one film writer. The soul of our group, however, was Moishe Broderson. Despite his dejection, his sense of humor never deserted him. One could fill a book with the comic ideas that he shared with us in those dark days. All our pain and anger found expression in his ironic observations, all the resentment and protest that we swallowed along with our rubbery bread.

In the most difficult days at that slave camp, when it seemed that all was indeed lost—when one Yiddish writer cried like a baby after I wrote down from memory a Bialik poem for him, which he kept hidden on his person like an amulet—in those days Moishe Broderson used to talk to us about Tlomatska 13 and his meetings with Yiddish writers there. He was the first to sniff out every bit of news about Israel that somehow reached us in this desolate wilderness. The Jewish State became Broderson's only hope and consolation. He carried the idea around in his heart as one carries a sacred scroll of the Torah, tenderly and with reverence.

When Pinke played Kol Nidrei

Since early childhood I have been in love with music and bewitched by its magic. Perhaps they were only fragmentary chords reaching me through the window of some well-to-do home in my shtetl, but for me those sounds could have been made only by an enchanting princess sitting at her piano.

The haunting Hasidic melodies that accompanied the fading twilight and the departing Sabbath—how deep was the yearning with which they filled the soul of a ten-year-old Hasid. For what, he did not know.

Later, as a yeshiva student in Warsaw, when I lived with my Uncle Moishe Dovid, his son Israel would come home from a concert of the Warsaw Philharmonic humming the sweetest melodies I had ever heard. It was then that I made the acquaintance of Beethoven and Mozart, Tchaikovsky and Bach, Verdi and Moszkowski. They sang within me and around me. I saw each day in terms of those harmonies that made me feel so good, so alive.

There was nothing I wouldn't have paid for the privilege of listening to good music. When I listen my whole existence becomes worthwhile. The whole world waits for me: it will not fall asleep until it closes my eyelids in blessed peace, like a mother who will not go to bed before she rocks her infant to sleep.

Then how did the musical instruments in this wretched slave camp become so accursed? Here they play only the strangest tunes as we are being marched out to work. And what are they, after all, those tunes? Melodies, notes written by creative composers. But within me they arouse fears that I suppressed in my earliest childhood. It was in Chekhotsinek, in the Polish spa for rheumatics, where my grandmother took me when I was six years old. Some lunatic there had dragged the Torah scrolls out of the synagogue and was defiling them. I attended the funeral of those scrolls, listened to the eulogies by great rabbis, and wept along with the thousands of Jewish mourners. Now here, in the camp, it was the melodies that were being defiled!

Captain Yermilov was deaf to the sound of music, deaf as the wall, but he kept a band at the prison camp because he received orders from higher up: music is good for morale —it increases productivity.

The band leader was a Ukrainian fiddler named Kuzmenko who probably had done all his playing at peasant weddings. Here he played for the prisoners as they paraded out to their day's slave labor to the beat of Mozart's "Turkish March."

The air is still ringing with the shouts of the convoy guards who escort the prisoners with machine guns and a dozen bloodhounds. They line us up in fives and bark out the order that is etched forever in our minds: "*Shag vpravo, shag vlevo—shtetayatsa pobyeg; konvoy prinimayet aruzhye bez preduprezhdenya!* A step to the right, a step to the left, is the same as attempting to escape, and the guards have orders to shoot without warning!"

So really, what does Yermilov need Pinke for, especially since he refuses to play that march for the prisoners going out to work? Pinke is a man of principle: he refuses to defile his violin.

Captain Yermilov cannot understand what makes Pinke so special. Pinke was second violinist and concertmaster of the Moscow Opera orchestra. When he was sent up, he brought along his 18,000-ruble Stradivarius. Of course he had permission, but the bookkeepers in the camp office barely were able to convince Yermilov that Pinke would be more valuable playing at the monthly camp concerts than chopping down trees in the forest. There was only one problem with Pinke—he was a Jew. Although his sentence —eight years at hard labor—is considered child's play in the camps, his crime was a dastardly one: Jewish nationalism, a crime for which so many other Jews were sent away.

How had Pinke come to be a Jewish nationalist? It seems that his brother, who had emigrated to America, wrote that he missed him and thought of moving back to Russia. Pinke quickly sent his brother a reply: *"Sidi i nye ripaysya*—stay where you are, don't budge!" Then Pinke made another fatal comment. This was at the time when the State of Israel had sent its first diplomatic representative to the Soviet Union, and Pinke simply couldn't hide his enthusiasm. Because of this our work assigner Niestorenko bore him a special grudge, this shameless Jewish nationalist!

Then again, our bandleader Kuzmenko envied Pinke his Stradivarius. He and Niestorenko used every trick in the book to make sure that Pinke didn't "hang around doing nothing, but should atone for his serious crime by working for the Soviet homeland." Pinke would not be sent outside the camp for work duty but would keep the barracks supplied with firewood. There was no reason he couldn't saw logs and chop wood; after all, it was the easiest job in the camps!

Dr. S., however, objected. Because Pinke's blood pressure was 210, the slightest exertion could be fatal. But Yermilov recognized only one sign of illness: exemption from work was possible only when the thermometer showed 37.6 degrees centigrade. Pinke had no temperature, so for five hours a day he chopped wood. By evening he was dead tired. After he rested for an hour, he would get out his violin and make it sing. Moishe Broderson almost would faint with delight when he heard the tones of that marvelous instrument.

"He's not number one, that Pinke, he's not a genius, but he's still a great master with an amazing technique. When he plays Paganini's 'Capriccio' you forget you're in a prison camp. He could coax the soul out of your body with that instrument."

Pinke would play, and we would stand around him in a circle and look at each other without recognition. Our padded overcoats with the numbers on the back, our shaven heads—it must be an illusion, some kind of cosmic error—a prince in beggar's clothing— the work of Satan himself. The heart swells, you begin to believe once more that all human beings are basically good. The evil ones? What does Scripture say? "The wicked shall disappear from the face of the earth." That Pinke and his violin!

Legends were told about him in all parts of the Taishetlag. "Have you heard Pinke play yet?" the prisoners would greet each other.

Pinke himself was a small, thin man with red eyelashes. A quiet, good-hearted person. One day I said to him, "Pinke, I'd be happy to work all night in your place if you'll only play for me, just once, Moszkowski's Spanish Dance no. 7."

"Nobody works for Pinke!" he protested. "I would never allow it!"

Pinke the Jewish nationalist was far removed from things Jewish. He didn't know a word of Yiddish. All his young life he had worked among Russians. He was a friend of the famous Russian singers Lemeshev and Koslovski. But you can never write off a Jewish soul. One day he thought up a plan: at one of his upcoming concerts he would include Bruch's *Kol Nidrei*. Pinke was a stiff-necked Jew. Hadn't he refused to play the marches that sent the prisoners out to work? Naturally Kuzmenko the bandleader was opposed to this strange musical number.

"*Shto takoye* Kol Nidrei?" he demanded angrily. "What's this *Kol Nidrei*?"

Pinke zealously defended his proposal. "If we can play

German music, then we can play a Jewish tune too sometimes!"

Pinke's Jewish number was a matter of contention for so long that it eventually reached the attention of the central office of the camp, where it was rumored there was a Jewish captain. After considering the matter thoroughly, the administration settled the issue by OK'ing the entire program as listed. Pinke was allowed to play *Kol Nidrei*!

Evening after evening, far into the night, Pinke practiced for the concert, as though he had a premonition it would be his swan song. This was a *Kol Nidrei* not in the appropriate autumn season, when the summer already has one foot out the door, when the leaves are falling and the winds sigh penitently within the human soul. No, this *Kol Nidrei* was heard in a snowy, frosty Siberian winter, six hundred kilometers from Irkutsk, in a remote slave-labor camp deep in the taiga.

Kol Nidrei.

There were some fifty of us—Jews of varying origins and education, of varying character and opinions. Among us were pious Jews from Samarkand and Lubavitcher Hasidim who, under the most difficult conditions imaginable, studied Torah and lived on bread and herring, refusing to touch the food cooked in the camp. Where did these Jews get the strength to do all that physically strenuous work? After a long day's hard labor, there they were, visiting others with a word of encouragement from the Talmud, a story from the Midrash, a miracle tale from Hasidic lore. If anyone offered to share something with them in return, they simply refused to hear about it.

Among us were also Jewish Communists, party functionaries who had worked with Lenin in the old days. After serving ten years in prison for Trotskyism, they had been rearrested and sent away again. There were well-known engineers who had built the finest bridges in the Soviet Union. And there were simple Jewish working people who hadn't been able to hide their feelings of joy when they heard the news about that modern miracle in Jewish history, the establishment of the State of Israel, and for this they were punished by long years of imprisonment, slave labor, and exile. And then there were Yiddish writers who had endured all the torments of investigation and interrogation but still were eager to bring the Jewish cultural treasures to their people in the language they had absorbed with their mother's milk.

These divergent Jews often quarreled with one another, patched up their differences, and then quarreled again. But on this day of Pinke's concert they all crowded together, tears streaming from their eyes.

Kol Nidrei. As if God's Holy Presence were consoling us here: Never despair, O my people, you have endured greater trials. You will overcome this one too.

And Pinke himself, who didn't know a single word of Yiddish, let his violin speak for him. All the generations spoke to us through his violin, comforted us, encouraged us, united us. Everything that had divided us crumbled and disappeared, and we remained children of one sorely tried people struggling to survive, hoping and believing in a brighter tomorrow.

That was Pinke's last concert.

With his high blood pressure, Pinke was not supposed to lift heavy loads, but the camp doctor had been unable to convince Yermilov of that. This was at the height of the Stalin terror; every scoundrel took the opportunity to lord it over us. Niestorenko, our work assigner, simply refused to excuse Pinke from hard labor.

One evening after work, Pinke complained of feeling faint. We helped him over to the infirmary, where he immediately lost consciousness. Two days later he was dead. The doctors diagnosed a brain hemorrhage.

Normally, dead prisoners were loaded onto a wagon like a sack of rotten potatoes, taken out to a field, and buried. This time, however, the Jewish prisoners were adamant: they were going to march behind the funeral wagon as far as the camp gate.

For this violation of discipline, a Yiddish poet from Bessarabia (whose name I can't mention), Moishe Broderson, and I spent three days in the cells.

Kuzmenko the fiddle-scraper couldn't wait to inherit Pinke's Stradivarius, but by various means we smuggled out a letter to Pinke's wife in Moscow, informing her of her husband's death.

Not until after Stalin died was she able finally to claim the Stradivarius, Pinke's hard-won Jewish fiddle.

The investigating commission

"*Komisovka* today!"

This is a scare word in the camps. Each camp is visited every three months by a special medical commission, a *komisovka*, consisting of free (nonprisoner) physicians. I went through dozens of such investigations. I came in an invalid and walked out able-bodied. For a short time I was reclassified all the way up to category 2; later I was reduced to 3 and 4. Each time it was either purely fortuitous or dependent on the mood of the doctor, most often a young woman fresh out of medical school.

Always, however, the local prisoner-doctors had a good deal to say about it, since they sat with every commission and their intervention could determine the prisoner's fate. This time we had no complaints. Our Ukrainian Dr. S. was not only a noted specialist but a great humanist, and he virtually waged war with the military doctors over each prisoner; this was especially so when Captain Nelga of the central camp hospital was on the commission.

Captain Nelga! The devil only knows why she was so mean. Perhaps it was because she got involved with the head of the convoy troops after the death of her first husband. Whatever the reason, she was constantly trying to reclassify prisoners from invalid to second class, which meant going outside the camp to do hard labor.

Most of these investigations were conducted in the camp bathhouse. We were called in by barracks. We undressed in the anteroom and waited in line. Everybody tried to avoid being examined by Dr. Nelga, but usually the work assigner was present and kept the line moving in order.

With Dr. Nelga cracking the whip, the commission this time made assignments across the board. All the invalids became able-bodied workers overnight. Third-category invalids (who were supposed to be used for light work, according to the regulations) were often exploited by the camp bosses; frequently these semicripples, mostly people in their sixties, were used for the heaviest kinds of work, along with first- and second-category prisoners.

I remember one case at camp 051 where seventy-year-old men were reclassified by a commission doctor to able-bodied workers. (Among them were the Latvian Social Democratic leaders Elias and Lawrence, who were not freed until 1955.) These older men were assigned to sawing logs, shoveling snow, and other kinds of hard labor. The same commission reclassified Moishe Broderson as able-bodied, ignoring his arteriosclerosis and a dozen other ailments. The next commission reclassified him back to invalid, but in the meantime he did his stint at hard labor.

Dr. Nelga also reclassified me as able-bodied, despite the fact that prison life and countless hours of interrogation had left me with unmistakable symptoms. Our brigade was split in two: invalids, who remained inside the zone, and able-bodied, who along with our brigadier Krushkin were sent to a renovation brigade. Our job was to repair the barrack dwellings of a small community of about fifty families near the camp. These were all employed in the camp administration as bookkeepers, accountants, expeditors, dispatchers, controllers, and telephone and telegraph operators; others were managers of warehouses for finished goods, materials, food products, and vegetables; the rest were camp administrators and convoy guards. Although all these people were on the camp payroll, they used the camp labor for their own needs absolutely free. We repaired their houses, cleaned up their yards—which were filthier and more neglected than those inside the camp—and kept them supplied with firewood and water year round.

At every turn we could see how rotten and degenerate this class of Soviet citizens had become. Idlers, illiterates, often without any skills whatsoever, this multitudinous parasitic apparat of the MVD lived at the expense of the Soviet people.

Inside the camp, the MVD officials used the prison labor for their own personal advancement and for the rewards they received for overfulfilled monthly plans. These incompetents earned their high salaries off the backs of the first-class skilled workmen, true masters of their craft, who did everything for them. The wives of this parasitic class never lifted their hands to do a stitch of work either. They drank right along with their men and passed the time with love affairs. Wife-swapping was common. The manager of the food warehouse was paying alimony to two women, but his business was running so well that he kept rising higher and higher in the system—after all, he had an endless supply of labor. The number of workers kept growing every day, and for a pack of tobacco they were ready to do whatever jobs were demanded of them. To whom could they complain?

The degeneration of this staff of MVD idlers and parasites can be seen from the large number of violent crimes they committed. In our camp a sergeant of the guards raped his own stepdaughter, a minor, and was given a ten-year sentence. In another camp, this one for women, the chief fell in love with one of the supervisors (a prisoner) and moved in with her. This was too much for his former sweetheart, a guard in the same camp, and she promptly reported him. The chief, outraged by this betrayal, waited for her one day after work and shot her five times. He was sent away for twenty years. Similar adventures were commonplace.

There were also a few good souls among them who,

like most of the Russian people, despised this class of oppressors and slave drivers. One day, as we were being transferred to another camp, our train stopped at a station to take on water. A detachment of regular army troops, waiting for a train on the same platform, practically showered us with bread, sugar, and tobacco. When our NKVD guards tried to stop them, a fight started. The commandant of the station —wonder of wonders!—took the side of the army men and refused to arrest any of them. Moreover, he held up our transport until he got an order from higher up, because he wanted it on record that the convoy guards had started the fracas by attacking the regular army soldiers!

When I expressed my astonishment over this sympathetic behavior of the simple Russian soldiers, one of the prisoners, an old Russian, said to me, "Why are you so surprised? Every single one of those soldiers probably has a brother, a relative, a friend, an acquaintance—somebody— who was or still is a prisoner in one of Stalin's camps."

Yes, we had the satisfaction of learning that Stalin's mania, his despotism and tyranny, had not managed to infect every Russian mind. The people knew about the injustices and sympathized with the innocent prisoners, but they were forced into silence by fear and terror. In the privacy of their hearts and minds, rebellion was brewing.

Avraham Khayim and the Sephardic Jews

To our Jewish colony in this bleak and desolate place a new element was added: Sephardim. They were arrested in the early 1950s—later than we—when the sentences were pouring out of Moscow like sugar from a riddled sack. Their sentences were stiffer than ours. Crimes that had been punishable by ten years in prison before 1950 were now all the way up to fifteen and twenty-five years.

Among these Sephardic Jews was the rabbi of Tashkent and a whole group from Samarkand. Most deeply etched in my memory is the saintly image of Avraham Khayim. His eyes still stare into my soul with a mute challenge, the same kind of look that glowed in the eyes of my teacher, Rabbi Meir Yekhiel Halevy from Ostrów, who fasted forty years for the sake of the exiled Divine Presence.

Avraham Khayim was neither a rabbi nor a scholar, yet his majestic appearance, his uncommonly handsome but gentle face, his deep, black, pensive eyes, cast a kind of awe even upon the non-Jews in the camp, who treated "Ravin Abraham" with reverence. Avraham Khayim was a toiler, a house painter who lived by the labor of his hands, but what a holy man he was! In the midst of all this evil and hopelessness, his glance was enough to ennoble us. He walked among us like a living Rebbe Moishe Leyb of Sasov, the great Hasidic leader.

In fluent Hebrew he told me about his crime. A few years earlier, a Lubavitcher Hasid had come to Samarkand and planted the seeds of Rebbe Shneur Zalman's teachings among some of the Sephardic Jews there. Avraham Khayim became a zealot of Habad Hasidism. His group studied the text of Shneur Zalman's *Tanya* and engaged in meditation. Avraham was even planning to install a ritual mikveh in his home.

Then, without warning, he was arrested. The MVD had evidence that he listened regularly to Voice of Israel broadcasts. Fifteen years! Avraham Khayim protested this outrage so vehemently that they added another ten. When I met him, this sixty-year-old, gentle man had twenty-five years in a prison camp to look forward to!

The other Sephardic Jews were there for similar crimes. Generally they kept to themselves. Aside from bread, sugar, and herring, they refused to touch any of the camp food, although our daily menu then consisted only of cabbage soup, two hundred grams of kasha, and three grams of vegetable oil. On Rosh Hodesh, the first Sabbath of every month, they would hold a prayer service. Since they were only nine men, they would enlist one of the Ashkenazic Jews who happened that day to be confined to the barracks by illness.

All of them were well into their sixties. Even a slave driver like our Captain Yermilov allowed them to work inside the camp zone, cleaning the barracks, helping in the kitchen, drawing water, and chopping wood. Prisoners who worked inside the zone usually could manage to buy a couple of hours of free time from the work assigner. The Sephardim received from home a delicacy that our local bully Niestorenko loved with a passion—dried Uzbek apricots— out of which his flunkeys would cook his favorite compote.

Avraham Khayim did not isolate himself among his Sephardim. When we returned from our daily labors exhausted, we would find him going from barrack to barrack, bringing something for each of us, and talking with us as if he had nothing else on his mind but our welfare. I often overheard his fellow Sephardim complaining to him, "What business do you have with those heretics?" But Avraham defended us; he had a good word for everyone. He loved to tell the story of Rabbi Akiba and Pupus ben Yehuda, who were both taken captive by the Romans. As they were being led away, Pupus exclaimed, "How fortunate you are, Akiba, that you are being imprisoned for studying Torah, and how wretched is Pupus, who is being imprisoned for nothing!"

When I said to him once, "My dear Avraham Khayim, we live in your merit," he objected angrily. "It is I who am the wickedest of the wicked! I deserve my suffering! You, however, are the grandson of a holy Jew. I am sure you will not die without penance."

This man knew all the Psalms by heart! Often he would write down a psalm for someone and say, "Here, look, you may be a freethinker, but just see what beauty is contained in these words!"

Once one of the prisoners received a package from home with some pork fat. As is the custom in the camps, a delicacy like that is shared with your neighbors. So one of us had the good fortune to taste a morsel of this rare treat. Working outdoors in the cold air, the body was starving for a bit of fat. (This happened a few years after Yermilov finally had put his camp in such good order that he relaxed enough to permit the setting up of a separate little kitchen, where prisoners could cook various things they received from home.)

For the Sephardim, this was a godsend. They could now cook the dried foods sent to them by their families. The separate kitchen was used by many Kazakhs, Uzbeks, and Muslims, who also did not eat pork. Here they were able to fry the mutton they occasionally received from home. So it happened that one of our Jews was frying the bit of pork fat that another prisoner kindly had shared with him. The Muslims complained bitterly to Avraham about this.

"Ravin Abraham, look what your Jews are doing!"

Avraham Khayim, the pious Jew, who himself fasted every Monday and Thursday and recited Psalms while he was working, smiled encouragingly at the guilty man.

"Pay them no mind! They're slanderers! For you it's a matter of *pikuah nefesh*, of saving your own life. You work hard outside the camp and nobody sends you anything from home. Go ahead and eat it."

The Jew was so overcome by Avraham's forgiving nature that he didn't have the heart to aggrieve the holy man by putting the pork into his mouth.

Our brother Sephardim were among the first to be freed from the camp. I don't know whether this was because of Moishe Broderson's appeals (which he wrote for them in flawless Russian) or because the charges against them were so blatantly false as to be ludicrous. Immediately after Beria's execution, when their appeals were reviewed, their sentences were reduced by twenty years. Persons with five years or less to serve were granted amnesty and released, along with their leader, Avraham Khayim.

The Jewish daughter from Riga

"Today is a special occasion for me. My one and only son is a bar mitzvah. Since he's not here with me, I have placed a frame of flowers around his photograph—wet with my kisses and my tears—on the wall in my corner. The Jewish women came by to congratulate me. We even arranged a little celebration. For several days we saved the best part of our meals for my son's bar mitzvah party, my son who is so far away from me. Who knows if I'll ever see him again."

Those lines are from one of the letters that a young Latvian Jewish woman (I'll call her Rosalie) wrote to us from camp 040, only three kilometers away. It required more effort and planning to conduct this correspondence than writing from Europe to America.

Camp 040 was a women's hospital in the Taishetlag (also called Ozerlag, from the words *Osobo Rezhimni Lager*, Strict Regimen Camp). Our camp had several contracts with 040. The stronger ones among us, particularly the younger men, were assigned there to do various jobs; we dug a well and built a new power station, for example. As usually happens with young people, no obstacle in the world could prevent the fellows from striking up acquaintances with the young women workers in the hospital. It was they, in fact, who brought us greetings from the several Jewish women who worked there, among them Rosalie from Riga, a pharmacist. For a pack of *makhorka*, one of the young men promised to find out for her the name of any Jew in our camp who came from Latvia. As it turned out, the only one answering that description was the Yiddish writer R.

Soon there was a steady correspondence between Rosalie and R. All the Yiddish writers in our camp took part in it. R. put all his talent into the long letters he sent to Rosalie. She wrote him back in a rich, literate Yiddish. Although she was aware of the devastation inflicted on Yiddish culture and its creators in our time, the flame of faith glowed within her all the more. I often felt that her letters were written not by merely a lover of Yiddish or a devotee of its writers but by a devoted mother consoling her children. Rosalie's name became a byword among us. Her letters were a subject of continual interest and discussion.

She reminded me very much of another woman I had met in my wanderings over the Soviet Union. In January 1942, the second year of the war, while I was working in a labor battalion, I landed in a military hospital in Novosibirsk after a serious injury to my eye. I was recuperating from a complicated but successful operation performed by a Jewish surgeon. Walking along a corridor one day I came upon a slender, aristocratic-looking woman staring out a window and obviously trying to choke back her tears. I started a conversation with her. When she learned I was Jewish, she broke down and unburdened her heart to me.

She came from Vienna. Her parents, strictly observant Jews, had brought up their highly educated daughter in the same tradition. When the Nazis occupied Vienna, she and her husband and baby fled to the Soviet Union. A few months later they were arrested and sent to a prison camp in Siberia on the charge of suspicion of collaborating with the enemy. They protested that they were Jews and had no connections with the Germans, but their pleas fell on deaf ears. In the camp her young daughter had a serious throat infection and was taken to the hospital. The mother was permitted to stay with the child, but under twenty-four-hour guard. Unfortunately, the doctors were unable to save her child.

Here it was Sabbath eve in this godforsaken place, and although it is forbidden to weep on the Sabbath, she could not stifle her lament. It seemed to me that this was how Rachel must have grieved for her lost children. The picture of that Jewish woman by the window remained vividly in my mind for years afterward.

We answered Rosalie's letters faithfully. When the camp discipline was tightened and the work brigades were searched as they left the camp and returned, we solved the problem by concealing the letters in the harnesses of the horses that transported our tools to the work sites.

There came a time when Rosalie began complaining in her letters about an X-ray technician in the hospital who was annoying her. He was a Ukrainian prisoner but not under constant guard. He told her he had fallen in love with her. As a pious Jewish woman, she rejected his endearments. At the same time, one of the camp bosses also was making advances to her. When she ignored him, he began undermining her position in the hospital by spreading false rumors about the quality of her work, even though her reputation as a pharmacist was outstanding. Her letters become more and more desperate but still proud and dignified, even when she learned she was going to be transferred to a hard-labor camp. Anything was preferable, she assured us, to being pestered by those two men and their declarations of love.

From her new camp she managed to send out letters to us until she was freed in 1955 under a new law releasing prisoners who had served two-thirds of their sentences and had a clean record. But being free did not mean going home. Most of the released prisoners were sent to Siberia as *pereselenets* (settlers). Although they were not confined in a camp, the territory of their exile was restricted, and they were forbidden to leave.

With the Chinese prisoners

For the Jews in camp 051, life was a daily struggle. In addition to the normal difficulties, we had to put up with the dirty tricks and insults of the Jew-baiters. On the rare occasions when a Jew was appointed leader of a work brigade, you could be sure they would look for—and find—some excuse to get him removed, even when, thanks to his ability, his brigade was earning a little more money and maybe not working as hard as some of the others.

For one quality, however, we were the envy of everyone else—our unity. True, we Jews often argued among ourselves, sometimes heatedly; we were, after all, individuals with widely divergent views, from God-fearing rabbis to veteran Communists. Some of the latter had learned something from their own bitter experience, but others, frozen in their old dogmas, still believed that whatever emanated from the top must be the quintessence of justice.

To the outside, though, we presented a united front— we pinched our cheeks and made them rosy, as the saying goes. Whenever one of us fell ill, the others saved part of their already meager rations for the patient in the infirmary. When one of us had a fight with the brigadier, for example, the Jewish tailors in the workshop intervened, and the man was transferred to another brigade before any injury could be done to him.

The other nineteen nationalities in our camp envied us for that. Even the well-organized group of Ukrainians were not as united as we were, although we could have learned a few things from them too: how to plan conspiratorially, how to keep a secret, how to conduct a strike, how to pull the wool over the boss's eyes. They were constantly fighting among themselves and would point to us as an example: "That's how to stick together!"

In this regard, the Germans were hopeless. Joint action with them was impossible. They always wore a smile and were friendly enough, but whenever some action had to be taken against the camp administration (after Stalin died, such things happened more and more often) you could never count on them. They were too accustomed to tight discipline. Just as they had dutifully carried out the orders of the Führer, so they regarded the rules of the camp boss as inviolable.

Another nationality that stuck together admirably and evoked the sympathy and respect of the other prisoners was the Chinese. Some of them had been wealthy men whose only crime was their allegiance to Chiang Kaishek, but there were also a good many ordinary people among them. Their ignorance of the Russian language left them helpless; they did not understand even the derogatory and abusive epithets hurled at them by sadistic overseers and brutish camp bosses.

In every camp I was in, the Chinese were put to work at their traditional occupations in the laundry and the bathhouse. Keeping the laundry and bathhouse running was far from easy. The workers there had to fetch their own water every day from the stream, and during the icy winter months this was hardly a picnic. They did their work quietly and with unusual efficiency. The bathhouse, the only pleasurable place in the camp, was always ready for us when needed. During those frosty days the heated bathhouse was the only place where prisoners could warm up. During the summer months, when the tiny gnats would cling to your skin and bite till your flesh swelled, the Chinese displayed their renowned patience particularly. Every evening after work we came to them in the bathhouse to help us wash off the sticky grease we had smeared on our faces. I never once heard them raise their voices to complain.

Very often the camp kitchen was left without a cook because all the cooks were terrified of the criminals and their forays on the pantry. At such times one of the Chinese would be transferred from the laundry to the canteen. They would have made first-class chefs, had there been anything for them to cook. Even so, they combined the few available ingredients into tasty dishes and managed to prepare something different every day. They would first cook and then add yeast to salted fish to produce a kind of marinated herring. The camp ration of oatmeal they would bake, cut into small slices, and dip in a brown gravy they somehow concocted out of flour. And they never refused a request to heat up the soggy bread that was doled out to us every day.

They even managed to handle the thieves, an activity in which their unity served them well. They simply worked out a schedule so that every evening the cook was protected by two bodyguards! The criminals took the hint and left the Chinese cooks alone.

One privilege the Chinese had in the camps was the opportunity to boil water for their tea. Since no tea leaves were available, they made something out of burnt chestnuts, which gave the hot water a chicory taste.

In addition to everything else, they had a delightful sense of humor. On cold evenings, whenever we would visit their teahouse to warm up, someone was sure to ask one of them, "And what are you in for, brother?" The answer had become a kind of ritual: *"Ya shpion!* I'm a spy!" Most of them in fact had been sent up for spying—and none for less than ten years.

The favorite Chinese of all the prisoners was seventy-year-old Li Fu, who once had been a high-ranking officer in Chiang Kaishek's army. Like many others, he was sentenced by Peking to serve his time in a Soviet prison camp. We spoke with him through former Russian émigrés from Harbin, Mukden, and other Manchurian cities, who were found in the camps by the hundreds.

Li Fu was a quick-witted man, keenly aware of everything that went on around him. A sort of Good Soldier Schweik, he even got the better of Captain Yermilov once.

The story was this. Despite his seventy years, Li Fu was still spry enough to do his share of work in the laundry, although his eyes were failing. His specialty was doing imitations of the interrogator who had made a "spy" out of him. His audiences would roar in appreciation, so it was hard to keep his imitation a secret. When Yermilov learned about it, he assigned this nearly blind old man to a brigade chopping down trees in the forest, which for Li Fu was tantamount to a death sentence. His fellow Chinese organized themselves and threatened to stop all work in the kitchen, laundry, and bathhouse if Li Fu was transferred to this hazardous job. Yermilov was compelled to admit defeat. The unity of the Chinese prisoners was simply too much for him.

Repercussions of the Jewish Doctors' Plot

How our work assigner Niestorenko suddenly got wind of the so-called plot of the Jewish doctors to murder Stalin only the devil knows. Nobody ever saw Niestorenko reading a newspaper. What did he care about such things? He needed newspapers only for wrapping the gifts he received from prisoners in exchange for exemptions from hard labor. Whatever newspapers came into the camp arrived days late anyway, and besides, Niestorenko made it a point to stay out of Charney's territory.

Charney was head of the DCE, the Department of Culture and Education. It was his job to arrange the camp concerts, to order the posters extolling Stakhanovite labor, to keep score in the socialist competition of the work brigades. Now and then he bought a book or two for the camp library. Primarily, he kept tabs on the packages we received from home.

And how closely he watched them! As soon as the post arrived with the packages, the DCE (with a guard present, of course) would begin their search for subversive material —letters, notes with suspicious codes. A code for Charney could have been anything, including a matchbox cover with the familiar picture of the Kremlin clock showing ten minutes to twelve. So what if these little boxes were manufactured and sold by the millions? Here in the camp they could have been among the secret signs and instructions for an escape plan, so they were confiscated along with all the other dangerous objects. But that wasn't the real reason for the search. The packages also contained good things to eat. People back home starved themselves to send their dear ones butter, cocoa, fruit. Here they were rare delicacies.

Anyone who has been subjected to interrogation knows that you can be charged with planning to set fire to the Kremlin, or intending to assassinate a Soviet leader, or being an agent of a foreign spy ring, and *dokazhi chto ti nye vierblud*—go ahead and prove you're not a camel! So when news of the Jewish Doctors' Plot reached the camp, all the anti-Semites crawled out of their holes. Jews are capable of any foul deed! These Jew-haters were practically ecstatic over the story. One Ukrainian nationalist was particularly incensed. "I knew that only the Jews could put an end to Communism—they started it in the first place!"

The hottest indignation, however, was displayed by those criminal offenders who inadvertently had been sentenced as politicals under article 58. The shame of it! They had to serve their time in the same place with Fascists who were trying to wreck the Soviet system! At every opportunity they dragged out their loyalty to the Soviet motherland. They became bosom pals with the citizen chief and gladly carried out his open and secret orders. In return, the chief appointed them squad leaders, work assigners, warehouse managers. Often they were permitted to let their hair grow long and wear their own boots instead of the galoshes produced in the camp's shoe factory out of old automobile tires.

For the criminal offenders, the Jewish Doctors' Plot was an unexpected piece of good fortune. "The *zhids*, the *zhids*," they kept agitating, "no wonder there are so many of them here! All this time we failed to notice them because their brother Kaganovitch protected them. Now their turn has come! This time we've caught them red-handed!"

It should be noted here that not all thieves are alike. There are various categories, and they are at perpetual war with each other. The honest thieves—the *chesnyokes*—stick to their time-honored code, which forbids collaborating with the enemy—the prison authorities—against other prisoners. They refuse to become brigade leaders, and they don't bother the politicals if the politicals don't bother them. The *urkis*, on the other hand, are those who play the role of reformed criminals. They never do any of the work themselves; they become foremen—and God protect the political who falls into the hands of one of that breed.

In our camp we had none of the *chesnyokes*, only *urkis*. Niestorenko, for example, our work assigner. Although he had been sent up as a political for collaborating with the Germans, he was on friendly terms with the *urkis*. He never assigned them to general work but put them in the easiest spots. For Niestorenko, the Doctors' Plot was a clear signal from above that now you could do with the Jews whatever you damn pleased, that the feelings you had kept under cover because you could never tell which way the wind might shift now could be displayed openly and without restraint. Niestorenko even arranged for copies of the Irkutsk newspaper to be brought in and distributed in all the barracks.

Inside Niestorenko's skull a diabolical plan was born: he would organize a separate Jewish work brigade. The Jews in the camps were not segregated. We had to endure plenty of nasty barbs, but all the nationalities in the camps carried the heavy yoke of their incarceration together. Sometimes this made for an exceedingly uncomfortable situation. A Jew could find himself sleeping in a bunk next to an SS man who had taken part in the slaughter of his nearest and dearest. That's the way it was in the camps—fire and water learned to coexist. A Turk next to an Armenian, erstwhile deadly enemies! A Frenchman with a German, a Ukrainian nationalist with a Great Russian chauvinist. They all had the same work norms and together they all sweated blood to fulfill them. Maybe there were people somewhere who would have liked to separate us, but they were afraid to do so. Now the signal had come right from the top—not only was it permitted to get the Jews, it was encouraged! There even might be rewards for doing it well.

So Niestorenko prepared a list of names for his Jewish brigade and turned it over to Yermilov for approval. Every Jew in the camp was on Niestorenko's list. Now he would show what he could really do. Even the older men would have to do their proper share—chop down trees, drag logs, dig ditches. Hitler was right. Jews should be outside the law! Our Captain Yermilov, who had no particular love for Jews either, was more a hater of *all* humanity, so he began by venting his spleen on our Ukrainian Dr. S.

Dr. S. loved people as much as Yermilov hated them. Despite all of Yermilov's threats, he continued to exempt as many prisoners from hard labor as he could under the circumstances. He told Yermilov bluntly, "You can do whatever you like with me, you can even put me on general duties with the other prisoners, but until you do that, I'll fulfill my function here as a doctor—to heal the sick, with medicine and the necessary bed rest."

Yermilov took this opportunity to let Dr. S. know that he no longer was a privileged character in the camp. "Soon we'll have doctors and professors here from Moscow, more than we need! Read the papers and see how many of those Jews already have been locked up. They'll all be sent here—straight into my hands!"

For the Jewish prisoners it was Tisha b'Av. We were in a special camp. When you land in one of those you can kiss your freedom goodbye. You finish one term, they slap another one on you. But to work in a special Jewish brigade was bad news indeed. It was clear from the outset that

Niestorenko was determined to make the Jews work harder than anyone else and to do it on less food. This undoubtedly would produce the result he desired: the cemetery near the wood across the railroad tracks would fill up with fresh graves, and the vanished Jews would be immortalized on the crude wooden markers—Y718, G387, R914.

But man proposes and God disposes. The Jew-hater was foiled, as in Haman's time, and we celebrated a new Purim, without *hamantashen* and *shalakhmones* true, and with watery cabbage soup and rotten oatmeal, but what a celebration it was! What a holiday in our hearts! To live to see this—it could only be credited to the merit of our fathers.

It happened because our camp and all the other camps around us were in an uproar. Our enemies became so involved with their own troubles that they simply forgot about us. In the interim our salvation arrived.

Concerning the moral standards of the camp bosses, who were supposed to rehabilitate us into good and useful Soviet citizens, we had seen more than enough. Not a week passed without a fresh little scandal in the free colony on the other side of the camp fence, where our guardians and providers lived. Stories about women who bloodied the noses of our bosses for not paying alimony were already commonplace. But now a certain lieutenant, a government official in the camp, started fooling around with a Ukrainian woman prisoner in a nearby camp. When one of his former sweethearts—a guard in the same camp—found out about this, she threatened to report him to his chief. Without thinking twice, the lieutenant drew his revolver and killed her.

The scandal caused such a turmoil that a special commission came all the way from Moscow and sentenced the officer to twenty years' hard labor. In the excitement surrounding the incident, Niestorenko and Yermilov forgot all about their plan for a Jewish brigade. And in the meantime, Pravda reported that the Doctors' Plot had been exposed as a frame-up: the doctors were completely innocent of all the charges.

So Captain Yermilov never did get his hands on the Moscow Jewish doctors and professors, and poor Niestorenko never had the pleasure of carrying out his Jew-hating plan. Furthermore, for attempting to set up a Jewish brigade Yermilov was reprimanded severely. Niestorenko fared even worse. He was removed from his post, and a commission came to the camp to investigate the whole sordid affair. As usually happens in such cases, as the threads began to unravel all of Niestorenko's larcenies came to light. He even had had some connection with the philandering lieutenant. Moreover, he was accused of seducing a loyal employee of the NKVD, the former administrator of the women's camp. Things went so far that they considered adding the charge of undermining the morale of the NKVD guards.

Niestorenko made one fatal mistake—he had moved too soon. Then again, was it really *his* mistake? In those troubled times, who could make head or tail of it?

300 women prisoners
from Mongolia

Out of the blue, like a sudden storm, a new affliction descended on our camp. All the prisoners in 051 were men. In some camps there were a handful of women inmates, but as far as the men were concerned, they were off limits. Merely talking with one of the women could get you two days in the cells.

One day three hundred young Mongolian women were deposited in our midst—sturdy, robust, sex-starved, blood pulsing fiercely in their faces and their full-blown bodies.

If anyone had asked Captain Yermilov whether he was agreeable to accepting that shipment of three hundred women his answer would have been a resounding No. They all had been convicted of robbery, banditry, or murder, and Yermilov knew from experience that such offenders have no desire to work, that they live off the backs of the politicals. But nobody asked him for his opinion.

Not far from our camp was a vacant site for about five hundred prisoners. Why this place was standing idle when all the camps in the area were crowded remains a bureaucratic mystery. The camp grounds were dirty and overgrown. Yermilov put in a rush order for a few hundred bunks from the carpentry shop. The new camp was under his authority as a sort of annex to 051.

When the transport of Mongolian women arrived, most of the prisoners in our camp were mobilized to help unload the trains. The women had been en route for almost a month. A massive brick cauldron had been built into one of the cars for cooking. This had to be dismantled brick by brick, stacked up, and later transported to our camp. The bunks in the trains also were taken down and carted away. We worked alongside the women, most of whom were younger and stronger than we; they soon outpaced us. Yermilov stood by, grinning. "Shame on you, you old dead-beats! The broads are working faster than you!"

Yermilov, who had developed a huge enterprise here—with our sweat and blood—and was continually taking on more and more projects, already had mapped out a plan of work for the new arrivals: he would set up a pig farm in their camp and cultivate five acres of land. He would open a workshop for making transparent plates out of mica. He would train some of the women to be wagon drivers and let them work around the camp; after all, they were not politicals, he didn't have to check every little detail about them with the higher-ups.

But right from the start they were a big disappointment to him. It began when two of our camp guards went to the women's camp and did not return at the expected time. These two guards happened to be real thugs who had harassed and terrorized the politicals at every turn, so we weren't sorry to hear they were missing. Nobody knew what had happened to them until Niestorenko confided to someone that they had been taken to the hospital more dead than alive. Those lusty Mongolian wenches had raped them and kicked them out.

This wouldn't have bothered Yermilov so much if those women only had done their share of the work. But they wouldn't lift a finger, even for their own comfort. One day he and his entourage visited their camp and warned them of the consequences of such behavior, whereupon the Mongolian women tore off all their clothes and screamed, "Give us some men first, then we'll go out to work!"

Yermilov barely made it out of there alive. He was so

alarmed by this turn of events that he even began to question the wisdom of the higher authorities. "Why do they send me common criminals in a camp for politicals?" (As if he himself didn't appoint gangsters as brigade leaders in his own camp!)

Soon a rumor was circulating that Yermilov was cracking up, that he was constantly banging his fists on the table and saying things like, "I'll write to Moscow! To Stalin himself! I built a model camp out of a wilderness! I saved the government thousands of rubles by using lousy cripples in my shops, and now they send me a plague like this!"

Every day there were new misfortunes. Here the women wrecked their bunks. There they knocked out the windowpanes. They threw rocks at the sentries in the watch-towers. The upshot was that for us regulars life became a little easier for a while. Yermilov rarely showed his face in the camp. He grew meaner than ever. As soon as anyone saw him coming through the camp gate, the alarm was spread in all the barracks: "*Yastreb idyot!* The hawk is coming!"

Yermilov became so busy with the women's camp that he had no time for anything else. In the meantime, Dr. S. tried harder than ever to excuse more and more prisoners from work for a day or two. Without Yermilov present, the work assigner and the brigade leaders were helpless. Fedko the clown entertained the men with stories about the troubles Yermilov was having with his own wife. Apparently he was not only hiding from us but from her as well. Day and night he argued with the central office to free him of the burden of "those women who refuse to do any work and who undermine my authority."

His wife, however, saw the matter in a completely different light. Right at the camp gate, in front of squads of prisoners, she berated him. "Always playing around with those tramps! Forgot all about his wife and kids! You bastard, if you don't come home now, this minute—"

Fedko described how our tough chief, who always

looked down his nose at the prisoners, followed his wife home like a meek little lamb as she filled the air with her choice language. "I'll scratch your eyes out, you son of a whore! I'll teach you to fool around with those tarts! I'll burn that whole damn place down with you and those bitches inside it—a women's camp he needs!"

The spectators held their sides with laughter. What sweet revenge! The chief himself! What a rare moment—to see with our own eyes the mortification of our tormentor.

Eventually Yermilov had his way. The three hundred Mongolian convicts were transferred to a camp on the Lena River. But Yermilov's sky had clouded. His throne had become a little shaky.

Stalin is dead

At first it was passed around as a deep, dark secret, furtively, from mouth to ear: Stalin was very sick. Not that we put much stock in this news from the other side of the fence. We were being tested constantly with such rumors. The bosses themselves would drop such bombshells and then check the reactions of the prisoners. They would monitor all the discussions in the barracks and record the comments in the prisoners' dossiers. Such provocations were especially designed so that later, when a prisoner finished his sentence, they could show him that even while he was serving his time he had continued his anti-Soviet agitation. Then they calmly took another ten years off his life.

This time we could read in the faces of our leaders that something extraordinary was in the wind. At first Captain Yermilov maintained the strict regimen of the camp, even tightening it. In the days when the secret news came, he put a special watch on the barracks to check who was not reporting for roll call. A practiced eye, however, could have noticed the panic in the behavior of the bosses. The chief himself, with his practical peasant intuition, had sensed that his authority was beginning to slip.

Then the day came when they could no longer hide the truth from us. All the sirens on the factories and locomotives blared during Stalin's funeral. Yermilov even compelled us to stand outside the barracks for five minutes of silence.

Afterward came the announcement of the amnesty. There were only a few candidates in our camp who could take advantage of the amnesty because it covered only those prisoners with sentences of five years or less. And the language of the amnesty law did not specify whether it applied only to criminal offenders or to political offenders also.

Novoye Vremya, the magazine that tries to be holier than the Pope, had not been ashamed to describe the State of Israel as the "center of international espionage." Now *Novoye Vremya* wrote that the amnesty applied only to criminal offenders because "there can be no mercy for enemies of the people." A few months later, however, the older politicals with five years left to serve were released one by one. At first they were not permitted to go to large cities, but later they managed in one way or another to be reunited with their families.

A thin ray of light appeared in the long, dark tunnel of our lives. The sworn pessimists among us who had insisted we were all doomed to die in the camps began to soften. A bit of hope arose that sooner or later an amnesty would be announced for our offenses too. The optimists were certain: better days were coming!

The same Yermilov who had tried to tighten the screws on us when Stalin died was flabbergasted totally by the execution of Beria, head of the Secret Police. The very next morning he was seen sneaking Beria's portrait out of the Culture and Education office. Then he wandered around in a state of shock, uncertain which path to take. Some of our wise guys even had the temerity to ask him, "Citizen Chief, how is Comrade Beria?"

Yermilov went about the camp sullen and silent, sunk in his own bewildered thoughts, hoping desperately for instructions from the top. Although nothing official came down—they weren't rushing into the breach with any proclamations about prisoners—various rumors did reach us that something good was being readied. The camp tailors, who had an in with the bigshots, told us that regulations were being written to release all seriously ill prisoners. This procedure, which was common practice for criminal offenders, had not been applied to politicals for a long time. Sick or old people, even those who no longer were productive, simply stayed in the camps until they died.

There was also talk that people who had served two-thirds of their time would be let out. Where did all this news come from? Was there anything authentic about it? Months later we learned that a special plenary meeting of the Central Committee of the Communist Party had adopted a resolution on prisoners after the uprisings in the camps at Kolyma, Norilsk, Vorkuta, and Karaganda, in which hundreds of people were killed. All this forced the authorities in Moscow to loosen the noose around our necks.

Yermilov, who always had said he couldn't stand weaklings, himself began to weaken. He startled people with his "Good morning" as he entered the camp. The discipline eased up. We no longer had to rise when a guard came into the room. One fine day, when we came back from work, the guards stopped us at the gate and began ripping the numbers off our clothing. Only the day before, at roll call, the foreman had given a couple of prisoners three days in the hole because their numbers were not clear enough; today he was running around like a lunatic tearing them off!

At first some of the men resisted. "These numbers are your shame!" they objected. "You yourselves are the ones who treated human beings worse than dirt! Let the numbers stay on as a reminder!"

They wouldn't even let us keep the numbers as a souvenir. For that infraction of the rules we were threatened with punishment. That same night they stopped the practice of locking us in the barracks at night. All these things were indications that soon we would be given the same rights as prisoners in general camps. The knot was definitely loosening. We knew that prisoners in special camps never had been treated like this before.

We also were allowed to spend the few kopeks we earned in the camp. Previously this money was credited to our account, and we needed the permission of the chief to use it.

Most important, the letters from home became more frequent and now contained words of hope. Stalin's death had brought a bit of cheer to the despot's slaves. There was talk that many of us would be sent somewhere else, perhaps to camp 046, which was much closer to Bratsk and civilization.

We are moved to another camp

After Stalin's death, our Captain Yermilov lost not only his former insolence, severity, and authority but his leading position in the camp hierarchy as well. Gone were the days when he could compete with the projects in any of the neighboring camps. He must have known he was losing his grip. He began making concessions to everyone except the workers in the central tailoring shop. He even halved the production norms in the shoe factory. His own invention, the rubber galoshes he had been producing in the thousands, had been declared officially unacceptable by the authorities. All the finished galoshes were ordered scrapped.

Rumors began flying that twenty freight cars were waiting at the railroad station to move prisoners to another camp. A new chief showed up to supervise the transfer. A short, stocky Ukrainian major with a potbelly, he circulated among us smiling knowingly and making promises to everyone.

"Stick with me, boys, and you'll lack for nothing. All I require is an honest day's work. I don't take advantage of anybody." With a gibe at Yermilov he added, "Even under the old regime I treated the prisoners fairly."

We started inquiring among friends to see which names were on the same transfer lists. The Jewish prisoners were especially concerned about this. It turned out that Yermilov had given away all the Jews in his camp to the new chief, keeping only a few tailors he needed for his production plans. Before loading us into the train, the guards lined us all up in the canteen with our bundles, which they then inspected with a fine-tooth comb.

The new camp was only twenty-six kilometers away, no more than an hour's trip, so why were they distributing rations for two days? Was the rumor correct—were we being sent all the way to Lena?

We did not go to Lena, but the trip was one of the worst I ever experienced in my years in the camps. For two days the train dawdled and crawled along that stretch of twenty-six kilometers. Despite the new winds that were blowing, the convoy troops treated us with their customary brutality. The cold was unbearable. The little pile of wood they had given us for the trip did not last very long. The sides of the cars soon were covered with ice. Normally such trains held thirty prisoners; now we were packed fifty to a car, with everybody pushing to get to the top bunks, where it was a bit warmer.

The general rule in the camps is that the lighter you travel during a transfer, the better off you'll be because you can move around more freely. I was one of the lucky ones; I was carrying nothing but two changes of underwear. I had no one on the outside to send me clothing, and whatever I had brought with me had been stolen long ago. I was able to fight my way to a top bunk. Moishe Broderson was much worse off. His wife had been sending him packages, and now he was carrying a heavy bundle. The prisoners on the top bunks refused to let him up, so for several hours he stood on the icy floor of the car. It was a pitiful sight, his tall frame bent over, freezing, immobile. I called to him to come up and change places with me, but he shook his head. Finally I managed to wrest a little bit of space for him in an upper bunk (and made a couple of new enemies in the process). He left his bundle below and climbed up with great effort. His long legs hung over the edge of the bunk as he held on for dear life. He refused to eat anything; he seemed satisfied just with this opportunity for conversation.

"Tell me, Emiot, how shall we ever write about all this when they let us out of here? All the accepted canons of literature, all the familiar approaches to the human heart, have proven false. What similes shall we use in our poems? Everything will sound banal, saccharine, and contrived compared with our actual experiences. For us they have killed the beauty of a sunset, the blueness of the sky, the bewitching sadness in a woman's eyes. And what about music? As much as I love Tchaikovsky, I'll never be able to listen to his 'Dance of the Young Swans' again without remembering how the prison orchestra played it. You recall that young fellow with the violin, and the two Tartar women with their accordions?"

The convoy train was resting on sidings more often than it moved. It would ride for half an hour and stop for three. During the night it slept. The salted fish we had eaten on the way made us thirsty, and we had no water. Among us were several men with stomach ailments. They kept running to the toilet—an uncovered bucket whose smells soon permeated the whole train. During the night the guards took several roll calls, but they couldn't be bothered to get us some water. The next day Broderson passed out once for a few minutes. I knocked on the doors for help; no one paid any attention.

After two such days and nights we finally arrived at the new camp. It happened to be a Sunday. The camp bosses were in no hurry on their day off to check us in. Toward evening they let us out of the cars. Thirsty and frozen, we were herded into an empty barracks. Evidently the building had been occupied previously by prisoners well enough to do hard labor. There was no heat. The first thing we had to do was choose a barracks foreman to get the stoves started. Moishe Broderson kept feeling worse and worse. I settled him into an upper bunk and went for the doctor. The doctor took one look, diagnosed it as pneumonia, and ordered Broderson taken to the hospital, where he lay in bed for two weeks.

Meanwhile, as was my habit, I moved around the camp with my eyes and ears open. It was a much smaller place than the one we had just left and considerably more neglected. Fimenko, our new chief, wasn't as concerned as Yermilov had been about the outward appearance of the camp. All he cared about was fulfilling the plan. He had his own particular approach to the prisoners—he kissed you while he stuck the knife between your ribs.

The camp project was to cut down trees for the construction of a small railroad station. On the very first evening Fimenko toured the barracks and talked with the men like one of the boys, bragging about his own democratic attitude, which he illustrated by playing dominoes with the men. Actually he drove us harder than Yermilov had, although he did it without insults or abuse. Part of his unique method was to go through the barracks preaching about the importance and nobility of labor. Only through the work record could the authorities determine whether a prisoner should be paroled after two-thirds of his sentence, as the new law prescribed. Many sick and weakened prisoners, who could barely stand on their feet, dragged themselves out to the work site every morning with Fimenko's words ringing in their ears: "Remember, the camp chief has a lot to say about who gets a release. In the end, it's his opinion that counts."

The secret agent and the bandit

In order to goad the prisoners into working harder, Fimenko had some of the men examined by a medical commission, charging they were unable to work and therefore of no further use to the camp. Most of the prisoners were not giving him any trouble; we did our work diligently, hoping for the privileges he kept promising us in return for good behavior.

After the uprisings that took place in some of the camps following Beria's execution, a number of new regulations were issued favorable to the prisoners. Visitors' privileges, for example. Fimenko set up a special barracks near the camp gate where prisoners could spend several days with their wives. He also announced that prisoners with outstanding work records would be permitted—upon his recommendation to the authorities—to reside outside the camp zone. It all depended on the behavior of the prisoners, meaning, of course, their work output.

Our new camp swarmed with an assortment of thieves, bandits, and cutthroats. Camp administrators who came to Fimenko for workers refused to have anything to do with these criminals, only a small percentage of whom ever did any work. Most of them had bullied the cooks into overlooking their pilfering of sugar, fats, and meat, which were rationed to the camp in small enough quantities to begin with.

The head of the Department of Culture and Education

in our new camp was a Jewish prisoner named Vronski. Until 1952 this Vronski had been a lieutenant-colonel in the counterespionage section of the Soviet general staff. He had been awarded nine medals and was due for a promotion to full colonel. In 1952, with many Jews being dismissed from the secret service, he had complained to a friend that this smacked of anti-Semitism. As a result of this one indiscretion, he was sentenced to ten years for anti-Soviet agitation.

Vronski kept sending appeals to Moscow. Because he had connections with the whole NKVD apparat, he was on good terms with the head of the secret police in the camp, who knew that with the way things were going, Vronski might be his boss some day soon. Vronski therefore was granted many privileges, despite his prisoner status, and soon began to show his true colors. He made friends with the leaders of the criminals, often inviting them into his office for a chat. He not only put them in charge of work squads and storehouses but gave them the easiest jobs and incited them against the politicals. He slipped into their way of life easily and began to speak their lingo. He let it be known that his mother was Russian—though both his parents were Jewish—and in truth he could tell an anti-Semitic joke much better than many of his new pals.

The Jewish prisoners of course despised and avoided him. The Ukrainians, for their part, kept sharp watch on him for a long time and then one day sent him an ultimatum: if he wasn't gone from the camp in an hour, they would see to it he went out in a box. Vronski appealed for help to the convoy guards, who managed to get him away safely. That was the last we saw of him. Until that moment Vronski did his best to make our lives miserable.

Not all the criminal offenders in our camp allowed Vronski to turn them against the politicals. I recall particularly a twenty-four-year-old gangster named Leonya Kostov, who had been sentenced to death four years earlier for killing five people during a holdup. His sentence, under article

59, labeled him a criminal offender, but when he got to camp he blurted out some antigovernment remarks and was transferred to Taishet as a political. During the few months in a death cell he apparently had searched his soul. When his sentence was commuted to twenty-five years' imprisonment, he decided to turn over a new leaf.

Exceptionally strong, limber as an athlete, Kostov overfulfilled his norm every day, no matter how hard the work. He had a good head on his shoulders. Most evenings he would play chess; he rarely lost a game. He never used foul language and seemed to gravitate toward the more educated prisoners to spend his free time with.

Leonya Kostov's bunk was next to mine. At first, before I understood his true character, I felt quite uncomfortable with this murderer for a neighbor. We became friends, and I spun many a yarn for him—fact or fiction—as he listened in rapt attention. When the camp authorities set up classes (at grammar school level), Kostov was the first to enroll. He worked hard to finish the six grades but still found time to tell me his life story.

Orphaned at an early age, he and his seven brothers and sisters endured much hunger and privation. For a brief period he was in a children's home; he was so badly mistreated by one of his teachers there that he ran away. He roamed the streets with other abandoned children until he joined a gang of criminals. Beginning as a pickpocket, he moved on to more violent crimes and served various terms in prison camps for minors. After each term he rejoined his gang and kept advancing in his profession until he became a leader. Finally, during a bank robbery, he shot and killed five people and was sent up for twenty-five years.

I wondered how it was possible, after so many crime-filled years, for Kostov to change so radically in character and behavior. Even his face seemed less hardened. The only trait that remained of his former life was his extravagance. He earned about six hundred rubles a month more than the rest of us but could spend it all in four or five days. He never sat down to eat by himself. He would buy a basketful of the best food from the camp store, set it all out on the table, and invite half the barracks to join his feast. In the camp dramatic productions he was always chosen to be the dancer and displayed his virtuosity in Cossack, Moldavian, and Polish dances.

We all knew that the chief of the Documents Section, a young widow, was not indifferent to Kostov's charm. She frequently came to see him dance and talk with him; she even tried to persuade the camp officials to reduce his sentence. For that matter, the wives of all the camp officials also came to Kostov's concerts. Whenever something needed fixing in their homes, they always specified that Kostov should do the work. True, he was a master of all trades, but the main reason was that women liked his company.

Usually, when he returned from one of these jobs, he was drunk and exuberant, and at such times the slumbering beast within him would awaken. He would burst into the camp kitchen, stick a big knife into his boot, and roar, "Today I've got to croak somebody—what about that rat Vronski!"

I had no particular sympathy for Vronski, but I did feel sorry for Kostov. When he was sober he was one of the most decent men in the camp. The only man I ever saw him hit while he was sober was an anti-Semite who was insulting a Jew. Whenever he got into one of his drunken rages I would stay close to him until I found an opportunity to lift the knife out of his boot and return it to the kitchen. Then I would talk to him, try to calm him down. Like a child, he loved to listen to stories; when he was drunk, this seemed to soothe him.

Since he overfulfilled his norm every day, Kostov had an excellent chance of being paroled in seven years. We used to worry, however, that in one of his drunken states he might carry out his threat to kill somebody, and then he would be doomed to the camps for life. We—the politicals—treated him indulgently, as one does a capable person who has gone bad for reasons beyond his control. Kostov evidently understood this and appreciated it; many a time he gave a brigade leader hell for mistreating a prisoner. One word from Kostov was enough to make the toughest squad leader think twice.

Even Vronski, who was afraid of him and tried desperately to get rid of him, granted him privileges reserved for special favorites. Vronski even arranged for Kostov's mother to visit him in the camp, whereupon Kostov decided to prepare a surprise for her that would bring a little happiness into her hard life. For this occasion he was given a room in the visitor's barracks. He whitewashed the walls and set up a little table complete with clean tablecloth and artificial flowers. Then he spent his whole month's wages and piled the table high with good things to eat. His old mother came with a gift from the kolkhoz—a loaf of white bread. When she saw the feast he had prepared for her, she wept for joy.

Our crafty chief Fimenko used this opportunity for his own purposes. He arranged a special camp meeting, with Kostov's mother as guest of honor. Then he made a speech about the successful "reeducation" in his camp, which had rehabilitated "that animal, Leonya Kostov," into a worthy member of the Soviet working class.

None of this, however, stopped the same Fimenko from later sending Kostov to another camp still farther away from his old mother. It was difficult to get at the truth of this, but Vronski must have had a hand in it somewhere. Knowing the interest the wives of the camp officials had in Kostov, Vronski arranged to have him sent to repair something in Fimenko's home. The prisoner was under guard in the normal manner, except that the guard stayed outside the house. What was going on inside was no concern of his; after all, it was the chief's own wife.

Unfortunately, Fimenko just happened to come home

early that day. What he saw going on between his wife and the prisoner remained a deep secret, but the next day Kostov was in a convoy headed for Lena. Not that it really bothered him very much, despite the distance. As he explained to us, "I only did it for one reason—to get even with that rat Fimenko for making a spectacle of me right in front of the whole camp. *He* was the one who 'reeducated' me, that lousy two-faced hypocrite!"

Celebrating the October Revolution

Once each year, on the day before November 7, the most important holiday in the USSR, the whole camp is in a turmoil. It begins with a general search of the prisoners' belongings for knives, clubs, iron bars—any object that can be used in a revolt.

Promptly at eight in the morning we are lined up outside the barracks, whatever the weather or the physical condition of the prisoners. (The cripples get down on the ground on all fours.) We form our ranks of five, and the guards, under the eye of the chief, search every prisoner. There are various kinds of searches in the camps. Our chief has his own system. The prisoner unbuttons his clothing down to his undershirt, no matter whether it's raining or snowing, and is subjected to a thorough search. The process takes hours. Lunch is postponed. Then all the prisoners are herded into the work zone, and the barracks are searched. Every stick of furniture is carried outdoors, even the brooms and snow shovels. The chief collects the trophies: needles, pins, pocketknives, and pieces of paper with writing on them. A poem written in an unintelligible language creates a furor and is locked away like a rare gem until it can be thrown into the fire.

Meanwhile, out in the work zone, the guards are taking a head count of the prisoners, once, twice, again and again, until the totals come out right. The census takers have to start over from the beginning more than once, because their arithmetic and their records are not the best, to put it mildly.

When they finally let us back into the barracks, it is late evening. Frozen through and through, we swallow down the cold, tasteless meal and then another threat looms: you may be a candidate for two days—November 7 and 8—in the BUR (pronounced *boor*). The difference between the BUR and the usual disciplinary barracks is that in the former you are permitted to take along your mattress and are given the normal food rations. The BUR is really a means of isolating those prisoners suspected of organizing some sort of strike, usually younger people who have shown signs of rebellion. If the foreman has a grudge against someone, however, he only has to drop a hint to a security guard, and the victim, no matter what his age, goes to the BUR.

Thus the seventy-year-old Laurence, a Latvian Socialist who had been locked in the Czar's jails and was now languishing in Stalin's, spent the entire holiday in the BUR. A fine, cultured man, he had earned the disfavor of a foreman by refusing to share his packages from home with this scoundrel, who bided his time until the opportunity arose to get even.

If you are lucky enough to avoid the BUR, you can attend a performance of Ostrowski's play *Innocently Guilty*, in which Hoffman, the painter, plays the mother. But before the play you are forced to listen to a long, dreary lecture by the camp chief, in which he proclaims that November 7 is our holiday too and that our temporary separation from society is really of little consequence. He explains to you how the October Revolution freed the working people from capitalist enslavement. Then he reads a list of prisoners with outstanding work records, and he juggles his words so as to create the illusion that you are now virtually a free man.

Our chief is shrewd enough to understand, however, that he cannot go too far, even on the Holiday of the Revolution. One camp administrator was brazen (or stupid) enough to hang up a banner reading, THERE IS NO OTHER COUNTRY IN THE WORLD WHERE THE HUMAN BEING BREATHES SO FREELY! It was not intended as a joke. Among the camp bosses there were enough abnormal people capable of such reasoning. In this case somebody higher up eventually realized that the slogan was ludicrous—if not invidious—in the context of a prison camp, and the banner was removed. But for those two days of the Soviet national holiday it hung there for all the prisoners to read while they breathed freely. (Didn't the Nazis display in the death camps their infamous slogan, ARBEIT MACHT FREI?)

After the holiday the prisoners were driven back to their slave labor. Many (including me) fell victim to cold and exhaustion. At long last I had the opportunity to lie in bed and not line up for work, but by that time I was more dead than alive. I spent several months in the hospital with an inflammation of the joints, and then Dr. S. persuaded our work assigner to transfer me to duties inside the camp area, explaining that I would never be able to march the three kilometers to and from the forest, nor could I move quickly enough to dodge the falling trees.

It took a whole week before they processed my transfer. During that time I witnessed the killing of an innocent prisoner by a sadistic guard for attempting to escape.

Shot while attempting to escape

It was common knowledge that in the special camps there was an unwritten regulation: any guard who caught a prisoner attempting to escape received a reward of five hundred rubles plus a month's vacation. We knew that the NKVD had its people everywhere. Even if a prisoner managed to escape, he would starve to death sooner or later, because appealing to a peasant or anyone else for food was a dangerous act in itself. Turning in an escaped convict meant a bounty of a month's supply of sugar. For these reasons no prisoner ever planned an escape attempt by himself. The ideal situation was a mass breakout, which happened only after Stalin's death.

Riskov, the guard in question (he was arrested later for raping his teenage stepdaughter), had a habit of bringing along a pack of dogs when he marched us out to work. Why did he need six dogs when there were six guards with machine guns? Only because he loved to watch a dog rip a prisoner's trouser leg with his fangs. The dogs were trained not to touch the leg itself, only the cloth. Riskov got a perverse satisfaction out of watching a man jump away in terror, and then he would fire his revolver into the air and call off the dog.

None of the other guards assailed us with as many obscene insults as did Riskov. Whenever he was in charge of the squad, we never walked to work; we ran in ranks of five, arms linked, and we had to stay together through the entire march. He never deigned to skirt a muddy field but plowed straight through it. Very rarely did he let you warm your hands at the fire. During the workday itself he never tired of reporting to the brigade leader the names of those prisoners who stopped to rest for a moment. On one such occasion I was a witness to his horrible cruelty.

We were chopping down trees. I had grown more or less adept at the work, although hardly a day passed without some injury to one of the prisoners. We worked in high winds, when it was difficult to judge which way a tree would fall. Every day there were accidents. The work area was delineated by markers stuck into the ground; beyond that line was off limits. One step into the forbidden zone could be interpreted by the guards as attempting to escape, and they were authorized to shoot.

If the guard was a decent person, we would make a deal with him to push back the work area so we'd have more room to move when the trees fell. Riskov, on the contrary, always tried to make the area smaller. It was a miracle that anyone in his convoy ever returned to the barracks alive. On this particular occasion Riskov overreached himself.

Yefimov, a good, honest man of about sixty, had been arrested for Baptist religious activity and sentenced to ten years' hard labor. I was with him for two years in camp 051 and never once heard him raise his voice. As though he were doing penance for some sin, he never missed a day's work, even when he was ill. Often he would help a fellow prisoner do his work or share his bread with him. Everyone in the brigade thought highly of him.

On this particular day we were startled by the sudden rattle of a machine gun. When we looked around, Yefimov was lying on the ground in a pool of his own blood—inside the work area. Almost at the same instant came Riskov's strident order, "Everybody—face down on the ground!"

When we stood up again we could see that the markers had been moved so that Yefimov's body was outside the zone. We protested immediately, demanding that a prosecutor be brought in. Riskov sent one of the guards for the doctor and the camp administrator. Then he ordered us to sit on the ground and threatened to throw the whole brigade into the guardhouse. "I shot him because he was trying to escape!" he screamed hysterically.

When the chief arrived, we all stuck to our story: Riskov moved the area markers after the murder so he could get the reward. The chief had no choice but to call in the regional prosecutor, and with him came a full commission. They paid little attention to our account of what had happened. Riskov emerged from the incident as a hero who only had done his duty. Because he had prevented the escape of a prisoner, he received not only five hundred rubles and a month's vacation, but a promotion to top sergeant!

Several of us were incensed enough to write to the regional camp administration, as well as to Moscow, protesting the commission's decision. The end result was that the chief came to us with a loud and bitter complaint. "Which one of you traitors dared to go over my head? I'll find out! And when I do, you can expect a transfer to a punishment camp!"

Apparently Moscow had returned our complaint with the one-word comment: *islyedovat*—investigate! Almost immediately the ritual began. All day long every man in the brigade was dragged individually to the DCE office and ordered to write a few words on a piece of paper, which was compared with the handwriting on the complaint. Naturally we all disguised our handwriting. The conspirators were never exposed. Our chief, still furious, disbanded our squad and dispersed us among other brigades.

This lawless killing of prisoners while attempting to escape was a common occurrence in those years all over the Taishetlag. Murderers like Riskov, wearing the insignia of the NKVD, were nothing but bounty hunters with hundreds of innocent victims to their credit.

We had to wait until Stalin and Beria themselves were

dead before we taught one of these sadists a lesson. Out of habit, one guard shot a prisoner under circumstances similar to the Riskov episode. We declared an immediate strike. The guard was tried and sentenced to ten years.

A Russian heart with a Jewish sigh

The camp greenhouse, in which I worked, raised various kinds of flowers, as well as seed for cucumbers, tomatoes, cabbages, and other vegetable plants. My wintertime duties were keeping the greenhouse heated at a steady temperature, fetching twenty buckets of water daily from the stream for the plants, chopping a supply of wood for the fire, and making and drying several hundred earthen flowerpots daily. During the summer I had to make twenty thousand of these pots, the peat for which is mixed with cow dung, ashes, and sawdust in a large tub. It is then shaped into the finished product with a tin can and a wooden pestle.

Of all the jobs I had in the camps, this was by far the easiest. Even though in wintertime we also had to clean the snow off the frames and cover them with mats every night and then stay up till midnight until a special watchman came to relieve us, there was really nothing to complain about. Summertime, of course, it was full steam ahead. Instead of twenty buckets a day, it was a hundred and twenty to water the garden and the hotbeds every evening.

In addition to all these normal duties, we had to wage a constant battle against the convoy guards and other assorted functionaries who used to stop by in the evenings to taste the tomatoes and cucumbers. The chief, who dropped in once a day to inspect the greenhouse, kept count of every tomato that hung on the vine.

Another frequent visitor was the ox, which was used

in the camp transportation system. This beast roamed freely around the work area and often stopped at the greenhouse to look down at the colorful vegetables twinkling up at him through the glass. He would open his eyes wide and—more than once the blood froze in my veins as I came upon that scene. That's all I needed—to have him fall in and ruin everything. How would we ever get him up out of there again? They would add another ten years to my sentence for sabotaging a state enterprise. How often I ran out of the greenhouse, grabbed that ox by the tail, and desperately dragged him away. He was not exactly a lightweight, either. When we complained to the chief about the animal roaming unrestricted around the camp, he replied, "You ought to be thankful to that ox for his shit. Without it you wouldn't be able to make your flowerpots. Besides, if you don't like it, I'll send you somewhere else. I can always find better workers for this job!"

I had no wish to leave the greenhouse, however. It was warm and peaceful there all winter. You didn't have to run out to the forest with a brigade and freeze all day long. It wasn't a dangerous job. And a tomato or two for yourself and your friends was a valuable asset. A few vitamins from a fresh vegetable was a real treasure in the camp, which was ravaged by scurvy.

For someone who had never been a thief, and for whom the act of stealing was repugnant, I must confess I developed a commendable artistry in robbing the greenhouse. I had to perfect two particular skills: first, to steal without compromising the manager of the greenhouse, and second, to smuggle the tomatoes and cucumbers from the work zone into the barracks without getting caught. I would hide the vegetables in my hat, in my sleeves, in my pants; the hardest part was to march boldly past the sentry post as if you hadn't a thing to worry about. At first, an unfriendly glance from the guard would make my heart pound, but I soon learned the art of mollifying the guards with a ripe tomato now and then so they wouldn't search me too carefully. It was worth the risk to see the joy and gratitude in the eyes of my friends and when I handed them the precious gifts.

The manager of the greenhouse was a renowned Soviet agronomist who had graduated from the Timeryazev Academy and had written several textbooks on the subject. Arrested in 1937, he had been in the camps ever since—more than fifteen years! Born of a Karaite father and a Jewish mother, he sang constantly at his work—a medley of Odessa pop tunes of the 1920s, most of them with a Yiddish flavor. At one time he had managed a large state farm, and he never wearied of telling us stories about his encounters with Soviet bigshots.

Despite his sixteen years in the camps, he behaved like a despot, imposing his views on his sixty-year-old assistant, Kucherenko, a Ukrainian Baptist leader. Although he had no formal agricultural training, Kucherenko had more practical experience than our manager. He had golden hands—everything he did was perfect and precise. He bore a deep hatred for our manager, whom he considered totally incompetent, notwithstanding all his education.

The manager, on his part, was furious with Kucherenko for his religious activities in the greenhouse, which he carried on quite openly. Regularly he would gather together his flock and preach his gospel. For this crime the chief administrator had threatened to fire him; since Kucherenko was a Ukrainian, and the Ukrainians were a majority in the work brigades, he hesitated to provoke them. Fulfilling the work plan—that was the primary consideration in the camps.

The manager resented Kucherenko for another reason: he had a better chance of getting out. The manager knew—and he reiterated it at every opportunity—that because of his Trotskyism he didn't have a ghost of a chance of being released. Ten years earlier he had been so sick and unproductive that they were ready to send him home; when they checked his file and saw what he was serving time for, however, they changed their minds. Even now, after he had served sixteen years of his twenty-year sentence, he still had no hope of a parole. Kucherenko, with his twenty-five year sentence, had a much better chance of returning to freedom sooner.

Despite his churlishness, the manager sometimes evoked my sympathy. Usually this happened when he despondently would take out the picture of his pretty Ukrainian wife and their two children, who were still tots when he had seen them last. Like millions of other Soviet children, they were being raised without a father. His daughter, a beauty with a pair of melancholy eyes, was now a first-year medical student. In the photograph, his son held a mandolin in his hands, though his weary, worried face certainly did not express any marked desire to play. Although he always tried to hide his partly Jewish origins, the manager never could restrain a Jewish sigh when he gazed at that photograph.

A Latvian of Jewish origin

This is the story of a strong, husky Latvian prisoner named Vidovicus, who looked like a German baron and turned out to be a Jew.

Because of the good work he did in the tailor shop's laundry, the administration overlooked his flowing mustache, a vanity forbidden by camp regulations. It was this mustache, which he trained carefully to curl upward, that gave him the look of a Teutonic squire. Hard as nails, he could fulfill two days' norms in one—work that was by no means easy. Our chief didn't get his monthly awards for nothing. His factory collected old, dirty, tattered pants and jackets and out of that raw material manufactured new clothing for the entire Taishetlag.

For this purpose these disgusting rags first had to be washed in the laundry. Then they were patched in the tailor shops. There were no washing machines in the camps. What did they need that technology for when there were plenty of human hands available? One of these hands was Vidovicus, who was almost a living machine himself. Where did he get the strength? True, he had a slight limp, but everybody knew that wasn't from weakness or rheumatism. It was a gift from his interrogator.

A fourth-year medical student at Riga University, he had come under German occupation and worked in one of their military hospitals. Vidovicus confessed that much himself; what was the sense of denying it? But the interrogator wanted something more from him, something about his connection with a Latvian nationalist organization. Vidovicus persistently denied this, so they beat him across the soles of his feet with a club until that splendid athlete became a cripple for life. Now he limped and walked with a cane, but he was still strong as an ox. After a hard day's work he would sit and pore over the medical books he had brought with him to prison. Most of his friends in the camp were Jews, and he always protested whenever he heard a Jew-hating remark. It was odd, this attraction that Jews had for him, a riddle that was not answered for me until much later.

All of a sudden, this giant of a man was felled like an oak tree by a stroke that paralyzed one side of his body. He waged a dogged struggle for his life. The other Latvians in the camp did everything they could for him, as did the Jews. He spent many months in the camp hospital. When he returned, he was a complete invalid.

One night he confided to me the secret of his sympathy for Jews. At the time I was also very sick, and my bed in the infirmary was next to his. The inflammation in my joints had finally disabled me. I ran a fever for days. My legs felt as if someone were drilling holes in them. My heart was weakened by the heavy doses of the drug they were giving me. For good measure, I also had fallen prey to scurvy. From the attitude of the doctors around my bed, I gathered I was not long for this world.

On this particular night, I already had awakened the doctor twice for something to ease my pain. I was reaching the limit of my endurance. It was then that Vidovicus told me his story. At first I hardly could make out what he was saying, but then, when I began to make sense out of it, I was so astonished that I forgot about my own pain.

When he was an infant during World War I, his Jewish parents fled from Riga along with thousands of others. In the crush, his parents lost him, and he was picked up by a childless Latvian couple. They baptized him, gave him a home, and brought him up as a good Christian. Until the age of twenty he never suspected that his parents were not his real mother and father. Since he had not been circumcised when they found him, it was not difficult to keep this from him.

Then, quite by accident, he discovered his real origins. His adopted parents suddenly had a falling out with their neighbors, who spitefully blurted out the whole story to him. From that moment on he could find no peace. As a Latvian he survived the Nazi occupation and even worked in a German military hospital, but he was fully aware of the horrors perpetrated on the Latvian Jews. Somehow he found ways to help a number of Jews in Riga escape the Nazi dragnet.

No one in the camp knew about his Jewish origins, but he considered himself a Jew. Whenever he could, he tried to make contact with other Jews.

When I had recovered somewhat from my illness, he and I talked for hours about Jewish history. His questions were insatiable. He asked me to teach him Hebrew. "I would like nothing better than to be a Jew openly," he sighed, "but if my Latvian friends here ever found about it they all would turn away from me."

I told him what the Talmud instructs Jews to say to any gentile who asks to be converted. I explained the bitter fate of the Jewish people in modern history. I tried to show him that to be a Jew requires endless fortitude. If the gentile is not frightened off by all that, says the Talmud, and if he accepts the Torah and is prepared to suffer for it, then and only then are you permitted to bring him closer to the Jewish people.

I don't know what would have happened with Vidovicus eventually. During the time we were together in the infirmary he learned a great many Hebrew words. He was extremely interested in Jewish customs and legends. I don't know whether he would have been able to make a full commitment to the Jewish people. Vidovicus suffered another stroke and lapsed into a coma. A few days later he died in the camp hospital.

Afterward, when I told Abraham Chaim from Samarkand about this, he could not forgive himself. "A Jewish soul lost among the gentiles! If only I had known, I would have brought his soul back to its origins, to its roots."

Tikhi

Without our own camp dog Tikhi, who shared our wretched lot in the Soviet prison system, our life would have been much drearier. Not that we lacked for dogs; we had too many of them. They were all of the wolf breed—tall and long, with thin, pointed muzzles and sharp, cruel eyes. Wherever our work brigades went they would accompany us. The convoy guards didn't trust their machine guns alone to keep us under control; they had a whole kennel full of dogs trained for tracking duty around the camp.

Tikhi, however, was *our* dog; we raised him for our own amusement. This was already after Stalin's death, and Yermilov, our ambitious chief, had eased up a little on the discipline. He was even ready to overlook an incident like stealing a puppy out of the kennel, especially since the deed was done by one of the best Stakhanovites in the camp, Grishka Fyodorov, who overfulfilled his norm every day by two hundred percent.

The story was this. One day Grishka's squad went out to chop some wood for the stoves in the kennel. While there, Grishka picked up a puppy, stuck it in his coat pocket, and brought it back to the barracks. He named the puppy Tikhi ("the quiet one"), in contrast to all the barking dogs that not only terrorized us by day while we were working but also kept us up at night with their incessant howling.

Tikhi was a newborn puppy; his eyes were barely open. Grishka fixed up a little box for him, lined it with absorbent cotton, and fed him powdered sugar in water. Tikhi was not exclusively Grishka's dog, however; the whole barracks adopted him, brought him gifts—condensed milk, honey, whatever delicacy came in the packages from home. In the gray, interminable monotony of our camp life, Tikhi was our only bit of cheer. We laughed at his comical antics as he crawled out of his box, ran around the room, tumbled over on his back, kicked his legs in the air, and squealed like a baby. When he grew, he ran all over the camp area, leaping playfully around the feet of the prisoners as they returned from the day's work.

Tikhi learned to eat the same food we did: black bread, oatmeal, even the *kapushniyak*, the cabbage soup we grew so tired of during those long years. When the animal was strong enough, Grishka began training him as a bloodhound. Eventually Tikhi was not only entertaining but very useful to us. First of all, he protected us against the criminal offenders who habitually harassed us, stealing whatever they could get their hands on in the barracks. Tikhi, who knew them all, attacked any one of them who tried to pet him or make friends with him.

Tikhi also learned to sleep during the day and stay alert at night, guarding us against thieves. Until three o'clock he would lie across the doorsill, and woe to anyone who tried to enter! Even our guards, with their red and blue NKVD caps, could not get past him; he seemed to recognize instinctively that they were no friends of ours and would bark non-stop until Grishka got out of his bunk and pulled him away.

Even our chief had a lot of trouble with Tikhi. One of Yermilov's rules was that whenever he entered a barracks, all the prisoners must rise. Tikhi would have none of this. As if to express our stifled protest, whenever Yermilov came in he always gave him a hot reception. Yermilov warned Grishka many times to retrain the animal, just as we were being retrained into obedient sheep who submitted to every command. Tikhi, however, refused to be reeducated. Even when Grishka tried to win him over with sweet talk about being a good dog and slapped him lightly on the rump (more for appearance's sake), Tikhi would give him a hurt look, as if to say, "Who are you kidding? Don't you think I know you hate that boss as much as I do?" Tikhi would choke down his barking, pretending he had swallowed something too big for his throat, turn up his nose haughtily, and crawl so far under a bunk that we hardly could get him out. Thus Tikhi demonstrated his displeasure with us all, with the whole world in which he could not detect a single grain of truth.

Then he would run off to Mikhail in the barracks across the way and offer his services. Mikhail, who was blind, had made a leash by which Tikhi led him wherever he wished to go. Tikhi had a special kind of love for this helpless young man. With Mikhail, Tikhi felt like a creature of some importance—independent and self-reliant. Whenever Tikhi guided Mikhail around, he became a model of good behavior, quiet as a mouse. His eyes would be fixed on the blind man, catching every turn, every nod, his tail wagging in pleasure as though he had just sniffed something good to eat.

But apparently Tikhi had his own accounts to settle. Who knows what thoughts went through his head as he lay there with his muzzle resting on his big paws, his eyelids drooping. One morning Tikhi stole out of the barracks and followed the brigade into the forest. No one noticed him on the way—he must have stayed far enough behind—but when we arrived at the work site, there he was, his hide shining like gray silk, his bushy tail stiff as a fox's, his eyes like two green flames, his ears alert to every sound for a mile around. Grishka, with only six months remaining of his ten-year sentence, was already dreaming about taking the dog home with him; he was ready to do battle with the bureaucracy all the way to Moscow for permission.

But Tikhi had other plans. First he had to get even

with Vostochin, the biggest, fiercest dog in the pack, who had torn the clothes off many a prisoner, sometimes drawing blood. More than any of the other dogs, Vostochin harassed us as soon as he heard a sharp word from any of the guards.

Tikhi began by giving Vostochin an innocent sniff. The other dog, his pride challenged by the insolence of this mongrel, turned on Tikhi and nipped him. Tikhi ran off among the trees, licking his wound and not uttering a sound.

Grishka sensed immediately that no good would come of this, but he could not chase Tikhi home without stepping out of the work zone into the forbidden area. In desperation he called "Tikhi, Tikhi!" For the first time in his life Tikhi disobeyed his master. A little while later, before anyone could stop him, Tikhi returned and leaped soundlessly at Vostochin, sinking his fangs into the other animal's throat with such force that it seemed he had been gathering all his strength throughout his entire obedient existence for this one life-and-death encounter.

Vostochin fought back valiantly, beat at Tikhi with his powerful paws, tore at him with his claws, but it was too late—his jugular vein was cut.

Grishka's face turned chalk white with the certainty that now Tikhi would never return to the barracks, let alone go home with him. A few seconds later we heard the rat-tat of a machine gun. This was not the usual playful firing that our guards loved to frighten us with; it was an act of vengeance against our dog. Our barracks would be a grim and cheerless place again.

Grishka and his friends stayed awake far into the night, scheming their own act of revenge against the camp bosses. Put ammonal in the kennels and blow it up? A pity on the poor dumb creatures, why take it out on them? Bore tiny holes in the cucumbers for the bosses' table and fill them with gasoline? No, they would know at once who had done it. The final decision was to pour hot tar on the back of the guard who had shot the dog. It would be done when they took us out to unload the supplies for the power plant. A delicate piece of work, but you leave it to Grishka. When it happened, it would look as if the guard had had an accident.

That was our revenge for the killing of our beloved Tikhi.

Rebellion

One of the favorite prisoners in our camp was Shil[
the Gypsy. No one ever asked him why he was in with [
politicals because we knew that the Soviet authorities did [
need much of a reason to put you in that category.

Shilam's wife and four children followed him to eve[
camp he was sent to. Shilam explained that this was a Gyp[
custom: wherever the husband goes, the wife goes with hi[
Young, raven-haired, her eyes black and burning, she visit[
him often. Somehow she was able to get by all the guar[
Every two or three days she brought him a package. S[
lived by telling fortunes in the surrounding villages. For[
years after the Socialist Revolution the Russians were st[
attracted to mystery and magic. Women still woke up wi[
dreams they wanted interpreted. Reading cards was co[
monplace, so the Gypsies had plenty of work to do, not on[
among the villagers but also among sophisticated city dwe[
ers. So many of the Russian prisoners in our camp woke [
in the morning with a dream to tell about that I knew almo[
all the signs. If you dream about a circus, it's a sign of fre[
dom; if you dream about taking something from a dead pe[
son, it's a sign of danger; if you dream about a rope, it's [
sign you'll stay in the camps. And so forth. This kind [
magical aura around the Gypsies, incredible as it may see[
intimidated even our bosses. They always gave Shilam t[
easiest jobs. His charming wife pushed her way past all t[
guards, and no one knew how she did it.

All this mystery paled into insignificance, however, when the Norilskers arrived. We had heard about insurrections in a number of camps, among them Norilsk, where three hundred prisoners were killed in an uprising. From the new inmates who came to our camp we heard exactly how the revolt broke out and what happened afterward.

Our camp administration prepared carefully for their arrival. The first thing they did was transfer the healthiest among us to another area in order to make room for the newcomers. They arrived one day in September, exhausted from the long journey. All of them were invalids, mostly Ukrainian Banderists who had taken part in the mutiny. Naturally we were eager to hear the details of this struggle between unarmed prisoners and a whole regiment of NKVD men with machine guns and tanks. The issues in the strike were the oppressive regimen in their camp and the brutality of the guards. To add fuel to the flames, the Ukrainians had learned that in a nearby women's camp the guards were raping Ukrainian women prisoners. They had received notes from the victims calling upon them to exact retribution.

The camp bosses at Norilsk—an isolated place where it stays dark for months and where the temperature goes down to fifty below—behaved like real dictators, driving the prisoners like slaves and then boasting about "the modern cities we are building in the frozen taiga." When the strikers put forward their demands for an amelioration of their living conditions, the camp administration refused even to talk about it.

A revolt broke out that lasted several days. The mutineers first killed the informers in their midst and then the work assigners who had been tormenting them with impossible norms in the quarries. They armed themselves with whatever weapons they could find—clubs, iron bars, bricks, rocks—and then they took rifles from the overpowered guards. Scores of prisoners were shot, but there were also

casualties among the guards. Then army tanks surrounded the camp, and the administration issued an ultimatum to surrender. When the prisoners refused, the tanks rolled into the camp, flattening barrack buildings with people still inside them, including many old and sick. Three hundred prisoners were killed.

An investigative commission came from Moscow and arrested the administrator who had ordered the tanks into the camp. The investigation found that the prisoners' complaints were real. Various compromises were proposed. Promises were made not to punish those who had taken part in the strike. (These promises were not kept.) The entire camp population was examined medically, and all the invalids were sent to our camp. They were a real problem for our chief. They refused to do any work. In the evenings their young men gathered outside the barracks to sing their national anthem. The big boss came down from the center to warn them, but one of them recognized him as the same official who in 1950 had said to a convoy of new prisoners, "Here you might as well dig your own graves. You'll see your own ears sooner than you will your freedom!"

The accuser publicly called this chief every dirty name in the book and told him to take his threats to hell. But everything remained the same, except that a new decree appeared in *Izvestia*, signed by President Voroshilov, releasing all those who had been sentenced for collaborating with the Germans; this was done on the basis of an agreement with the Adenauer government in West Germany. The Voroshilov amnesty meant that those who had served in the German army but had never been part of any punishment squads were amnestied immediately. Those who had committed their crimes as civilians had their sentences reduced by half.

The mood of the German prisoners soared, even though their general situation had been improving anyway. Now they expected their freedom any minute. This naturally caused much resentment and grumbling among the other prisoners, who complained, "The Nazis have more right to an amnesty than Soviet citizens themselves!"

It was common knowledge that most of the prisoners in our camp were serving ten- to twenty-five-year sentences for crimes that were not even grounds for arrest in countries where law and judicial process prevail. There were also prisoners who had murdered Jews and other people for the Gestapo or who had worked as guards in the death camps, and their sentences were no longer than those meted out for expressing anti-Soviet opinions. These murderers, who had been writing appeals all along proving they had nothing to do with the Nazis, now did a complete about-face so they could fall within the amnesty for collaborators with the Germans. One of them asked our camp administrator, "I killed only two Jews. Does that make me eligible?"

They are assembling the first groups of Nazis to send home, most of them former Gestapo men. But there are also some ordinary Germans who were brought here under suspicion of espionage for the United States. One such seventy-three-year-old man, a clockmaker, was sent away for ten years on the charge of espionage because his daughter went out a few times with an American officer.

Then comes the turn of the Ukrainians who had served in the Germany army. Very few of them were freed, because they had been in the special killer squads.

Negative replies began coming in from Moscow to the appeals of Russian citizens. Resentment was building up over this amnesty covering Jew-haters and depraved hoodlums. But then something happened that united all the prisoners in our camp.

All the politicals had one common demand: we wanted the criminal offenders separated from us because they were constantly stealing and starting fights. It was the practice among politicals to leave their personal belongings out in the open; they were not in the habit of taking things that belonged to others. The criminals had no such compunctions; not a day passed that something wasn't stolen from the barracks. They did their work so skillfully that the watchman never caught them at it, so it was he who took the brunt of our complaints.

The new prisoners from Norilsk, however, who were exceptionally well organized, set traps for the thieves, caught them red-handed, and roughed them up. A few days later they learned that the criminals were sharpening their knives in preparation for an all-out attack. There were some twenty of these gangsters; we had been complaining steadily about them to the camp chief, but he turned a deaf ear to all our appeals. Aside from their thefts of property inside the camp, they also stole dogs outside the camp area, slaughtered them, and ate their flesh. Most of the other prisoners were appalled and disgusted by this practice.

The primary aim of our strike was to get rid of these criminals. It was not an easy struggle. The administration was traditionally on their side. They never tired of insisting that they were loyal Soviet people who were only fighting against the Fascists, as they called the politicals.

By sheer weight of numbers, we drove them out of the barracks. They pulled out their knives and counterattacked. We overpowered them and tore off their clothes. They retreated all the way to the camp gate, where the guards fired a few shots in the air. The chief came running with his armed lieutenants. There weren't enough of them to stop us, however, and he couldn't get help from other parts of the camp because the same thing was going on there.

He refused nevertheless to yield to our demand. His own prestige was at stake. Particularly furious was our work assigner, a degenerate criminal himself. He fired his revolver point blank into our ranks, wounding one of the men. This so enraged the strikers that they sent an ultimatum to the guards: get the criminals out now or remove their corpses tomorrow.

The administration granted our demand, but only temporarily. A few days later they sealed off the camp, and the guards conducted an investigation to find the ringleaders of the strike. Not only did they fail to uncover any names, but we warned the work assigner that if he wanted to stay alive he had better get as far away from the camp as possible. When the camp bosses realized that this was turning into a general strike throughout the Taishetlag, they sent an urgent plea to Moscow for help. Moscow's reply was simple and direct: handle the matter yourselves; we are too busy now with more important problems.

During the strike we were threatened with transfers to more remote camps, but we paid little attention to them. It was the criminals who eventually were transferred, not the politicals. After this success we were less timid about calling a general strike over the next grievance. Normally such activities would be considered sabotage, and the punishment would be swift under article 58. But the good old days were gone. The prisoners no longer could be so easily intimidated.

The trigger for the next action was a hunger strike declared by a Polish prisoner named Strykowski. During the period of the Polish government-in-exile under General Sikorski, he had been named to represent the London government in the Krasnoyarsk region. As soon as relations between the Soviet Union and the Polish government-in-exile were broken off, he was arrested by the Russians as a spy and sentenced to ten years' hard labor. Later he was transferred to a special camp in Siberia, where the commandant immediately confiscated his Polish documents and listed him as stateless. Strykowski protested that he had not one but two legal documents—a Polish identity card and a diplomat's passport—but it was no use. Several months later he was found guilty of organizing a mutiny against the Soviet army, and another ten years were added to his sentence.

This unfortunate Pole lost four fingers of his right

hand during his incarceration. Despite that he continued to work and later was assigned to manage the agricultural projects in the camp.

When rumors began circulating that the foreigners in the camp might be released, Strykowski wrote appeal after appeal to Moscow as well as to the local administration. All the replies he received were the same: he was a stateless person, not a Pole. Strykowski declared a hunger strike in protest. On the fifth day of his strike the doctors tried to force-feed him. In his support, the prisoners declared a sympathy strike throughout the camp. Again the administration had to admit defeat: Strykowski would be included among the foreigners eligible for amnesty.

May it get no worse

In our difficult life in the prison camp, we grew accustomed to almost everything. One eventuality still frightened us, however—a transfer to another, more distant, camp. I had a personal reason to fear this. During the last *komisovka* I had been reclassified in the second category, which gave the administration the right to do whatever they wished with me. Bosses from other camps came to our chief regularly whenever they needed men for especially hard labor. I had escaped all these selections because the chief usually chose prisoners who were unproductive; he was only too glad to be rid of them. The only protection against this was to be known as a good worker, but where could one get the strength to keep this up year after year?

I had in fact become a physical wreck. Day in, day out I went with my work brigade to unload heavy sacks of flour, sugar, and other products from incoming freight cars. What would my mother have thought if she had returned from the grave and seen her only son—whom she had raised to be a rabbi—carrying sacks from the cars to the scale (a distance of 150 meters) and then hoisting them up to be stacked in the warehouse?

The work norm for the second category was six tons a day. Your son, dear Mother, fell to the ground under the weight of the first sack he tried to lift. Then two of us tried carrying it and learned that if you hold a sack of flour in your arms—even with two people working together—you can rupture yourself. It's much easier to carry it on your shoulder by yourself, once you've learned the trick of getting it up there.

But now your son is too weak to carry a ninety-kilogram sack of sugar. I am not blaming you, Mother, for not training me to do that. How were you to know that one day I would be a slave laborer in a Soviet prison camp? You must be turning the heavens upside down, urging all my ancestors to persuade the Most High to forgive my sins and grant me the strength to endure such vengeful punishment.

Whenever I'm late returning to the barracks in the evening, Moishe Broderson runs all over the camp looking for me, afraid that something terrible has happened. Such happenings are a daily occurrence in the camps, yet when I ask him what he wishes for himself, he sighs, "Only one thing: I hope things don't get any worse."

Yes, we were all afraid of that "any worse." We knew very well what those special camps were like. From that kind of camp they usually carry you out feet first, and no one knows where your grave is. From that kind of camp you never return, even if you live long enough to serve your entire sentence.

Moishe Broderson and
Sholom Aleichem

Early in 1955, when the discipline had eased a little, we heard that the Artists' Brigade from a neighboring camp system was on a concert tour and soon would be visiting us. Such brigades traveled in special trains and enjoyed special privileges: they could dress fashionably, they did not have to shave their heads, in some cases they were not under constant convoy guard. Most of the actors were professionals who had become entangled in the Soviet prison system for some political sin.

Our camp never granted such privileges to its inmates. In the early fifties, before Stalin's death, even renowned engineers and doctors were compelled to do general camp work such as digging ditches, hauling sacks, sawing logs, and chopping down trees. The fact that the camp administration was now permitting a traveling Artists' Brigade to visit us was a sign that the reins were indeed slackening.

This Artists' Brigade consisted of six men and four women, all professional actors from Moscow and Leningrad repertory theaters. One of the women, a comedienne now in her middle years, was a highly capable, sensitive actress. The other women were younger: a Ukrainian popular singer, a Tatar accordionist, and a violinist. A concert like this was first of all a noteworthy event for the camp employees themselves—all these pretty women in the camp at one time! Before the program there would be a reception for the actors in the big barracks of the Department of Culture and Education, and the actresses were not averse to a little harmless flirtation with the young men. The full kitchen staff was mobilized for the occasion. The foremen went among the prisoners, collecting delicacies from home—white flour, sugar, fats, cocoa, sausage, chocolate—anything the chefs could use to brighten up the usual lackluster menu. From somewhere a set of glassware appeared—"human dishes" we called them, as opposed to the regulation wooden bowls. The meal was brought into the room on a tray covered with gleaming white cloths.

We Jews in the camp were especially interested in the young violinist from Latvia, whom we had heard much about from nearby camps. Even the anti-Semites had nothing but high praise for his artistry. His face was remarkably fine and sensitive, as if his years in the prison camps had left no traces whatsoever. He had come to Siberia in 1940 as a young boy with his entire family, who was exiled for the sins of his wealthy father, an industrialist. Right from the beginning the lad had shown real talent. Graduating as a physicist from a Siberian university, he had displayed such extraordinary musical gifts that he was accepted to a conservatory.

Then the ax fell. For membership in an illegal Zionist youth organization—he was caught listening to Voice of Israel broadcasts—he was sentenced to twenty-five years' hard labor!

The young man was extremely interested in the Jewish prisoners in the camp, particularly the Yiddish writers. We invited him to our barracks and introduced him to Moishe Broderson, who embraced him as if he were his long-lost son. We could not stop marveling at the way he had been left unscathed by the coarseness and ugliness of prison life. He told us that through all his years in captivity he had continued his studies. He read his books diligently on the train while they were traveling from place to place. He begged us to lend him whatever important books we had among our belongings. I immediately went to Professor S., who had accumulated a good-sized library, and told him about this studious young man. The professor gladly selected three philosophical works as a gift. The violinist was so moved by this that he made a little speech.

"My dear fellow Jews, I have not yet told you about the most precious possession I brought with me, a small book printed in Yiddish. I would find it extremely painful to part with this book. It is Sholom Aleichem's beautiful story, *Shir Ha-shirim* (Song of Songs), published by the Moscow State Publishing House before the recent pogrom on Yiddish literature. I've read it more than a dozen times. Whenever I don't have the time to sit and read it through from beginning to end, I turn the pages just for the pleasure of looking at the Yiddish letters. Many Jews in the camps have begged me for the opportunity to look at this book. I cannot even think of parting with it, but I will gladly lend it to you so you can copy it over, and the next time I come here you can return it to me."

We assigned this sacred task to Moishe Broderson and the writer R., both of whom had a clear, graceful handwriting. By this time a number of newspapers and magazines were allowed into the camps, but to copy a Yiddish book was still a risky business. Some overzealous guard might catch you at it and, not understanding what it was, might tear it up or turn it over to the office, where it would be studied interminably. So the copying had to be done late at night, hidden from prying eyes.

Broderson had been fired from his duties as night watchman. With his irrepressible humor and his fertile imagination, he constantly was creating new epigrams and puns about the camp bosses; this was the only way he could get even for all the degradations and insults suffered by sensitive people in the camps. When his jokes eventually reached the ears of the bosses, he was fired from his good job. But it was 1955, when men his age who were classified as invalids no longer could be forced to do hard labor. He had his own upper bunk, where he would lean against the wall for hours, reading. There, in secret, he began tenderly copying out Sholom Aleichem's *Shir Ha-shirim*. The work was later completed by R.

The joy this manuscript brought to the Jews in the camp is indescribable. It was the first Yiddish book we had seen in years. The copy passed from hand to hand. I recall how the writer Gertz-Movshowitz forgot all about the heart condition that was keeping him chained to a bed. Unable to contain himself until the copy could be brought to him, he put on his clothes and walked all the way to Broderson's barracks to look at the printed Yiddish words with his own eyes. Enslaved Jews read Sholom Aleichem's words and laughed through their tears.

All this was thanks to a wonderful, talented young Jew from Latvia, one of many such unsung heroes in the struggle for modern Jewish culture.

On the eve of liberation

A medical commission arrived at the camp to release those prisoners now completely incapable of doing any physical work. The commission designated three categories: prisoners who still could work, those about whom there was some doubt and who would be sent to a hospital for further examination, and the sick and disabled who obviously no longer were capable of working. Moishe Broderson was placed in the third group, I in the second. For a period of many more months, Broderson was not freed and I was not sent to a hospital.

The procedure required that, in addition to the medical examination, one had to appear before a legal commission consisting of a judge, a prosecutor, and a representative of the camp administration. This commission did not come to the camps very often, and without their certification, people like Broderson simply had to wait. His wife pestered the authorities in Moscow for so long that our chief received a telegram from the General Prosecutor's office ordering him to send Moishe Broderson to a hospital for examination. One month later I was sent to the same hospital.

It was a warm autumn day when I left the camp. Although we were escorted by two guards on horseback, the discipline now had been greatly relaxed. Moreover, the guards knew they were transporting people who were seriously ill and they therefore were not worried about our attempting to escape. Actually we were supposed to make this trip inside the wagon, but since it was too crowded and I was still well enough to do so, I walked behind the vehicle.

One of the guards was a young Jewish fellow from Odessa. To his credit, let it be said that he didn't push me too hard, no matter how far behind the wagon my weakened legs lagged. Every once in a while he would ride back on his horse to see if I was still there, but he made no attempt to hurry me along. I began to taste the sweet air of freedom for the first time in many years. For most of the day I walked along without any guards in sight, without the sound of machine guns and barking dogs. I began to notice the beauty of the forest once more. Among the pine trees I could see an occasional birch, its leaves announcing the approach of fall. The birds in the trees were worlds removed from the evil around them; they carried on their courtships exactly as they had been doing since Creation, and they serenaded each other ecstatically. From deep in the forest came a fresh breeze that caressed me with promise-laden secrets. How pleasant it would be to sit down here under a tree and daydream awhile. And apparently that's what I did, because suddenly a guard was shaking me, pretending he had been looking for me a long time.

We had traveled ten kilometers. Six more to go. It wasn't such a long distance, but how weary I was! How badly my body had been battered during those long years in the prison camps. My heart raced, I couldn't catch my breath, my legs were swollen. Summoning up my last ounce of strength, I stayed on my feet until we reached the hospital.

That evening I was examined by several doctors, supposedly for my bad eyes. The head of the commission, a captain, put his stethoscope to my chest; from the expression on his face, I sensed that something was seriously wrong. In an incredulous tone he ordered me to lie down and rest for a while.

"You walked the whole way? You must have done it on purpose—to speed up your heartbeat!"

After I had rested he listened to my heart again and told me to get a good night's sleep and report to him in the morning. In the meantime, they X-rayed my chest and took a cardiogram. The captain didn't trust the technician—he supervised the procedure himself.

In the morning I met Moishe Broderson in the hospital corridor. He had been recuperating here and was only now on his way to the commission for examination. The captain examined this sick, broken man for a whole hour to make sure he wasn't faking. To Broderson's objection that he already had been examined twice and twice had been put on the invalid list, the captain quipped, "*Bog troytsu lyubit—*God loves things that come in threes!"

The third examination revealed that Broderson was suffering from thrombosis in his legs, from sclerosis, and from angina pectoris. Finally they gave him the exemption, but even this did not spare him from being dragged in a convoy to the Molotov camp. All the exertion worsened his condition still further. Later, when he was in Poland, his death came suddenly.

When my turn came and the doctor examined me again, he was merciless, apparently because of my comparative youth. Notwithstanding all the new winds that were blowing, the authorities were reluctant to part with a prisoner before they had squeezed the last bit of strength out of him. They still needed cheap hands for hard labor. The doctor's ultimate diagnosis of my condition was impaired vision, a weakened heart, and swollen legs resulting from previous inflammation of the joints. Even after he discharged me, the captain, not completely satisfied, called me back to check my blood pressure again. Luckily for me, it was over 200.

Finally I was sent back to the camp to wait for the legal commission, which alone had the authority to release me on the basis of the medical commission's report.

From Moscow came more and more replies to prisoners' appeals. Examining judges arrived in person to conduct reexaminations. Prisoners recanted their own previous testimony, claiming they had been tortured into giving it. The judges didn't bargain very much; they merely wrote down whatever the prisoner said.

Among those released at that time was Dr. G., a nutrition specialist from Moscow, who had supplied special food concentrates for Professor Schmidt's expedition to the North Pole. The story of his arrest is another one of those incredible instances of the Soviet legal system. It seems that Dr. G.'s young bride had wanted to get married during Passover. The celebration took the form of a seder, which they arranged for their friends. During the seder, Dr. G. apparently had called out, "*L'shono ha-bo-o b'yerusholayim*—next year in Jerusalem!" Among the many invited guests at the holiday party must have been one informer. His report to the secret police characterized the seder as a Zionist demonstration. Dr. G. was charged with Jewish nationalism.

Through all his years of incarceration, Dr. G. worked in the camp kitchen as a consultant to the chief cook. Now he was packing up his belongings with a big smile on his face, as if the years he lost in the camps were a big joke. His fellow Jews in the camp accompanied him to the gate with the wish, "Let's hope Ahasuerus doesn't go crazy and order Vashti to dance naked on the table." Yes, the fear that Ahasuerus might go crazy again and lock up millions of innocent people still haunted us.

In the meantime, releases were arriving every day, and every day there were new rumors: all the camp bosses were busy learning new trades; the entire Taishetlag would be liquidated and all the personnel fired; one of the chiefs already had quit and taken a job on a collective farm—he didn't want to wait until the last minute, when all the good positions would be filled.

Farewell to Moishe Broderson

When a commission suddenly arrived to transfer some of the prisoners to the remote Molotov camp, Moishe Broderson said to me, "They've gone crazy. It's plain as day. They don't know what they're doing."

It was true. The camp administration obviously was knocked off balance by the most recent rulings. Life had been so simple for them during those last seven or eight years—everything going according to plan; a steady stream of prisoners entering the camps; the regimen continuously being tightened; the camp bosses, undisputed rulers, doing whatever they pleased, undaunted by the complaints and protests of the prisoners. Each camp boss merely tried to corral the healthiest, strongest people for himself, and when these slaves became weaker and less productive, he had no trouble finding new ones.

Now that system was upset. The bosses knew from experience that after some time had passed the camps would have a full complement of hands again. Such things happened in the Soviet Union with dependable regularity. There was nothing to worry about, things would return to normal soon. But what were they to do in the meantime? The camps were emptying out gradually. Every camp was pressuring Moscow for permission to draft prisoners from other places. Naturally, what counted most here was the importance of the projects in each camp.

The Molotov camp demonstrated successfully that its

chemical plant was more important than our lumber yard. It therefore was granted a permit to recruit more hands. When our administrator protested that he would have no one left to do the work, the authorities advised him to go to other camps and do his own recruiting.

As Broderson said, the big bosses themselves must have become irrational. Why else would they have started selecting cripples from our camp, men who had been designated incapable of doing a day's work? When such prisoners complained that they would be going home soon anyway, the reply was, "From Molotov you won't have as far to go."

Then suddenly I learned that it was possible to avoid this new *komisovka*. Even though the chief himself had ordered everyone to report to the Molotov convoy, he was really much more interested in having the prisoners stay behind with him. No one was looking forward to this long journey to the new camp anyway. I suggested to Broderson that he take his time about reporting to the medical commission. He was already so fed up with the whole business that he reasoned it would be easier for him to get his release once he was in the new camp. "At least," he consoled himself, "Molotov is not a special camp."

True, during the 1940s and 1950s, political prisoners in the special camps would have jumped at the opportunity to transfer to Molotov, where there was a regular work regimen, where you didn't have to wear numbers on your back, where you could write as many letters home as you wished, and where you were not ruled so despotically. But now the discipline in our camp also had been relaxed, and most important, we lived with the hope that at any moment the order would arrive to send us home. I therefore decided to stay where I was and not appear before the medical commission. Most of the other Jewish prisoners made the same decision.

I said goodbye to Broderson as he was leaving with the

transfer convoy to the Molotov camp. What would he do there? The commission doctor told him, "Don't worry. There are hundreds of trades there you can work in—even dollmaking!"

That was all Broderson needed. "I'm going off to make dolls!" he announced, with that unquenchable humor that never left him, even during the worst moments. It was enough to look at his haggard face, his bent back, the deep sorrow in his eyes, to grasp the bitter irony in his words. As I helped him carry his bundles to the gate I felt a deep foreboding, and I tried to etch his features into my memory.

That was the last time I saw him. After our four long years together in the camps, how much pain and degradation we had endured together! I have felt always that if I remained spiritually unbroken, if I didn't lose my mind, it was only thanks to Moishe Broderson, who at the worst moments supported me, encouraged and comforted me, cheered me with his keen observations and clever gibes at the Soviet prison system. In his presence I almost forgot my own hopeless situation. Through our tears we said goodbye to each other for a long while.

My premonition was all too accurate. A short time later, on his way to Israel, Broderson stopped in Poland, where he died of a heart attack.

Moishe Broderson was not one of the executed Yiddish writers, but his ordeal in the Soviet prison camps undoubtedly hastened his death. And he was not the only one.

Soon afterward, I learned that Rabbi Lev, head of the Jewish community in Kharkov, had died in a camp hospital. My acquaintance with Rabbi Lev was a brief one—we were shipped to different camps—but even in that short time I learned what a fiery Jew he was. He fairly bubbled with Torah and Jewish learning. Others told me of his battle with the NKVD, who followed him day and night until they finally trapped him, tried him behind closed doors, and sentenced him to ten years at hard labor. He did not survive.

In the village of Stepanovka

Those of us who remained in the camps were moved to location 010, where they kept all the prisoners about to be released. Here the discipline was so relaxed that they permitted us to leave the camp area after the working day was over. All we had to do was report our comings and goings every day to the watch.

The camp services had been sorely neglected, however. Since we were not sent on contractual labor outside the camp zone, the administration did not assign anyone to take care of the daily necessities. Previously there had been a women's camp here working on a special project; it was exempted from providing its own firewood, which was assigned to another camp close by. After the women were transferred, the barracks were abandoned.

Now we had to go out to the forest to chop our own wood and to the stream to draw our own water. Since these duties were not on the list of paid jobs in the camps, no one wanted them as a regular chore. The mess hall therefore remained unheated and the cooks were replaced every day. The meals were erratic and the bread was frozen. Still, we had the satisfaction, after so many years, of moving around like free men. We could go out to the nearby villages, talk to people, and observe life in this far corner of Siberia.

Two kilometers from the camp, across a frozen river, lay the ancient Russian village of Stepanovka, where you could still find some people whose parents were born there.

The men still wore their flowing long beards and the familiar peasant caps. There was a kolkhoz in the area, but the older folks delighted in talking about the good old days when they drove their troikas to Taishet and bought enough food and kerosene to last all winter.

The peasants in Stepanovka welcomed us warmly. Their chief complaint was that, because their village was inadequately supplied with medical services, they had to turn to Dr. Levanda, the camp physician, whenever they took sick.

The village clubhouse was filled with the new potato crop, so the young people gathered in the evenings at the storefront office of the Agricultural Administration and danced to the tunes of Misha's accordion. It happened that Misha was preparing for his wedding with Katya, a sixteen-year-old village beauty. Peasants whispered to us that her mother had served time in the camp and that Katya had been born there, but no one knew who her father was.

Half the prisoners in our camp were invited to the wedding. Katya's mother, still young and pretty herself, greeted the prisoners more affectionately than she did the officials of the kolkhoz. She had a big Russian heart and treated us royally, although she knew she would have to go hungry the next six months to pay off the cost of her daughter's wedding.

Many of the men from camp went to Stepanovka for a day's work on the collective farm. Since they were paid by the day, they didn't have to wait until the end of the year for an accounting, as did the kolkhoz members. While they were there in the village, they found cozy places for themselves in some household. In no other place in the world, it seemed, were there so many widows and lonely women as in Stepanovka. Some prisoners were hoping to settle in the village. First of all, they had no one left back home; some who had served many long years in the camps lost their families during that time. Second, while everybody wanted to go home, the fear of being arrested again still lingered, and the less visible they kept themselves the better off they were. The Ukrainian prisoners found places in the surrounding woods among Ukrainian families who had been exiled at the end of the war and by dint of toil and perseverence had made new homes here.

Every six kilometers along the railroad line stood an overseer's hut. The overseers—all of them women—had very specific duties: winter they cleaned the snow off the tracks, summer they tried to prevent accidents. Each day our young fellows would return to the camp with boastful tales of their conquests among these railroad girls.

The wife of one camp administrator ran a store near the camp, where she sold all sorts of scarce goods and expensive cigarettes, or items the free population could not buy, such as moldy sausage, rancid preserves, and—most desirable —whiskey diluted generously with water. Some of our fellows, who recognized her as a former overseer in a prison camp, recalled that she once had punished an inmate by tying her to a tree and letting her stand there so long that her toes and fingers froze.

Now she was all sweetness and smiles. The men found ways to make her life miserable: broken windows in her store, a dead cat in a tub of honey, a fire the night watchman put out just in time. Then men used to ask her, "Sophia Nikitichna, what will your husband do when all the camps are shut down?"

"It will never happen," she retorted, "not in our lifetime!"

"But there's an order out already, Sophia Nikitichna. The camps will be empty. Your husband the major will have to become a sheepherder in the kolkhoz."

The village children follow me around wherever I go.

How long since I've heard the innocent laughter of children! The snow is deep. I join them in their games of tag. The children have grown fond of their "uncle" and want to go back with me to the camp. The guards will not let them in, so they stand outside the fence, call to their *dyadya*, and refuse to obey their mothers' summons to come home.

Vitya Kasoka, who had served two ten-year terms in the camps, was expecting his wife for a visit. He looked like a walking skeleton. His friends tried to spruce him up, lent him a suit, a shirt, a jacket, anything to make him look more presentable. The barber gave him a special haircut, even sprayed him with a double portion of cologne free of charge. The men kept encouraging him, building him up for the meeting with his wife, but the next morning he returned a defeated man.

"My wife is sorry she ever came here. She doesn't want to take me home. In these twenty years I lost my manhood too."

Letters keep arriving at the camp, sad letters, from prisoners who have returned to their homes. People harass them, look upon them as criminals. One writes, "In the camps at least I could say what was on my mind. Here I've got to keep my mouth shut."

The effect on the prisoners is to make them more and more despondent as their day of freedom approaches. From several ex-convicts we hear that their families have turned their backs on them: an extra burden. After all, they had come home fatally ill.

The village of Stepanovka meanwhile was doing everything in its power to turn the situation to its own advantage. The women of the kolkhoz practically threw themselves at the prisoners. In their loneliness they came to the camp laden with gifts. Our chief became a matchmaker. Obviously it was in his interest to keep as many men near the camp as possible.

A reply finally came to the appeal I had sent to Moscow a year and a half before. Paragraph 11 of article 58 was to be removed from the charges. According to paragraph 10, section 2, my sentence would be shortened. I was therefore eligible under the amnesty declared by the President of the USSR on March 27, 1953, and I was hereby released.

My sentence never was annulled completely. Soviet justice could not permit itself to go that far. They only removed paragraph 11, that is, the charge of participating in an anti-Soviet organization. My punishment thus was reduced to five years. I had already served seven. Should I demand compensation for the extra two years?

As soon as the order came from Moscow, I was sent to another camp where I would be completely free and would not even have to report every evening. Strangely, there I met my onetime work assigner Niestorenko, the unconcealed anti-Semite who had caused us so much grief in camp 051. He had been promoted to the document section. Evidently our curses and ill wishes had not hurt him one bit. Afraid to return to the Ukraine lest someone testify against him there for his crimes during the Nazi occupation, he settled in Chuksha, in far-off Siberia, found a woman who agreed to marry him, and lived a dissolute life there with the rest of the camp bosses.

In Chuksha we were allowed to use the library and to go to a club where they showed films occasionally. In short, we began to feel more and more like free men. The procedure for preparing our documents was so drawn out that it took another two weeks. Each document had to be completed in five copies, which we then had to take to the head of the regional militia for our passports. When all that was finished, we had to go to Taishet for the railroad tickets and food rations for the journey. Taishet swarmed with thieves and pickpockets, who tried to relieve the newly released prisoners of their last few possessions. The trains were full, and again we had to wait three and four days for a seat.

My first destination was Khabarovsk. The trip there took five days and nights, for which I received three rubles a day expenses. This barely paid for bread and tea, but who cared about that? It was February 1956, and I was a free man.

Back to Birobidzhan

The journey back to Birobidzhan is not made in a Stolypin car. If it weren't for my typical prison-camp jacket, my grimy, padded pants, and my shoes too big for my feet, I could have passed for an ordinary Soviet citizen. True, on the shelf above my head is not a suitcase but a plain burlap sack with my remaining personal belongings, but people in the Soviet Union are accustomed to seeing this, especially since there are so many others on the train who have just been released from a prison camp. Passengers who hadn't served in the camps aren't much better dressed, particularly on this railway line.

Not that our political-prisoner uniform is anything to be ashamed of. The free Soviet citizen is sympathetic to us. Everyone I speak with on this train has either a close relative or a friend who served time in the camps. In fact, one feels a little freer on the train than at home, where the secret police are everywhere. Tongues loosen and people unburden their hearts. Passengers ask about imprisoned relatives from whom they have not received a letter for years. Men weep, remembering friends who died in the camps back in 1937–38.

All day long the train plods ahead through the hills. Lake Baikal is still there. The Russians call it the "holy sea." They sing songs about it and spin legends about it. Long ago, on our way out to the camps, we hardly noticed the beauty of the lake. If anything, the prisoners prayed that the train would jump the rails and tumble down into the water.

Now, however, I look out at this Russian sea in all its majesty. It seems as deep as the Russian soul, which you really cannot fathom; one moment it is kind and gentle, ready to do anything for you; the next moment, enslaved by satraps, it is capable of perpetrating the worst horrors upon itself and upon others.

Finally I am back in Birobidzhan. I entered the city, still asleep beneath the deep snow, as a wintry day dawned. When I walked into the Birobidzhan Hotel with my burlap bag, the manager, a woman who knew me before my arrest, was overjoyed to see me. The first thing she wanted to know was if I had been rehabilitated or only amnestied. How splendidly they oriented themselves here regarding the difference!

She was correct, that woman. The fact that I was still not rehabilitated caused me a great deal of trouble during those few months. Everyone treated me with distrust. By that time, many of the returned prisoners had been granted full rehabilitation. The Yiddish writers from Birobidzhan, however, were only amnestied. Their crime—attempting to introduce Yiddish culture artificially into the Jewish Autonomous Region—had not yet been exonerated, and their sentences were cut in half.

Luckily, a friendly Jewish engineer found a minor job for me in the Birobidzhan clothing factory. It paid three hundred rubles a month, which turned out to be enough for only ten days' subsistence. I rented a room in the home of a poor Jewish family. My landlady lived in one large room with her seventeen-year-old son, who worked in a furniture factory; his wages were not enough to support both of them, so she did odd jobs to make up the difference. I slept in a corner of the kitchen, for which privilege I paid one hundred rubles a month, one-third of my wages. I was glad to have the job—checking the cloth for imperfections before it went to the cutters. I also checked the material for correct measurement, which meant I had to lift the heavy bolts. After it was cut, I delivered the cloth to various crafts in the factory for further processing.

I was truly grateful to my landlady for my living quarters. On one pretext or another, fearful about my ex-convict status, no one else had wanted to take me in. The two hundred rubles that remained after I paid my rent barely lasted ten days, but I made peace with my fate. Compared to what I had gone through in the camps, now I was living like a king.

My landlady was proud of her other sons, who were married and had good jobs. Only her daughter was not with her. A young Jew from Poland had fallen in love with her and taken her away with him to Israel. The daughter wrote letters home every month, but her mother was afraid to answer them.

"Believe me," she explained. "I'm not afraid for myself. I'm worried about my children. Ever since they arrested so many Jews here, I don't even trust myself. Still, I couldn't stand it any longer. Last month I wrote a letter to my daughter in Israel. Nothing special. Just that my health was all right and that I didn't need any help from anyone. Who knows whether I should have done even that much?"

I tried to reassure her. I advised her to listen to the radio, which after the Twentieth Congress of the Soviet Communist Party was full of reports about Stalin's "errors." Meanwhile, she found the courage to remove Stalin's picture from its prominent place in the room and hang it up in my corner of the kitchen.

Many familiar faces had vanished from Birobidzhan since I was arrested in 1948. It was rumored that these people had fled the region. Certainly many former Jewish officials had been replaced by Russians. But Reuben Stein, the Lithuanian Jew who had done more than any other person to keep the city green, was back at his post. Many new parks had been added, new buildings had been erected, the entire four miles of Sholom Aleichem Street now were paved, and the buses rumbled back and forth from one end to the other.

People no longer stood in line for bread; food products were relatively plentiful. But the former centers of Jewish culture were utterly lonely and forsaken. Almost against my will my feet took me to the courtyard of the former Yiddish theater and the surrounding homes in which so many Yiddish artists had once lived. The actors had dispersed to all corners of the Soviet Union. The theater itself, which recently had been renovated, was now a Home for Pioneers. A gifted Jewish soprano now sang Russian tangos during intermissions at the movie house.

The four-page Birobidzhan *Star* was printing Yiddish translations from the work of Andrei Possar, a young poet of the Far Eastern Nanei people. This rather unprolific poet now lived in Birobidzhan in a comfortable apartment provided by the authorities, and the Khabarovsk Writers Union had managed to send him to Moscow to study at the Literary Institute. Mostly he wrote about the fish that his national group (a few thousand people) caught and made available to the rest of the country. Why were the Jews of the Soviet Union any less important, I kept asking myself over and over.

A new government bookstore had been opened in Birobidzhan, selling books published in every language spoken in the USSR. Only one section was missing: Yiddish. For appearance's sake they had put out a few old Yiddish pamphlets, yellowed and crumbling. The manager of the store, an honest Russian woman, could not understand this. Puzzled, she asked me, "Have all the Yiddish writers stopped writing?"

Among Jews in Birobidzhan

Spring 1956. I am a guest in the home of Bumagin's daughter. When I was arrested eight years ago she was still a schoolgirl. Now I am holding her child, the grandson of a hero. I remember vividly the day I received a telegram from Mikhoels to do a story on the family of Hero of the Soviet Union Joseph Brumagin, who had worked in the Birobidzhan wagon-making factory.

I found Brumagin's family at that time living in poverty in Smidovich. His wife recently had suffered a terrible ordeal: her child fell beneath the wheels of a maneuvering locomotive, and her own hand was crushed in the same accident. I still recall the thousand-word story I wired Mikhoels about this simple man of the people who was killed in the war against the Nazis. Brumagin was decorated posthumously and awarded the title of Hero of the Soviet Union. In my telegram to Mikhoels I quoted a sentence from his last letter to his children. Their father was about to go out on a mission that would "bring honor to the Jewish people and avenge my brothers and sisters murdered by the Nazis." He instructed his children to let his action serve as an example for their own lives.

Later I proposed to the authorities that the Autonomous Region appropriate a sum of money to support his widow and young child. A whole block of houses in Birobidzhan was named in his honor. Thus I became a friend of the family, and now Brumagin's daughter had invited me to her home. Since the wave of arrests, however, people were more reluctant to talk than ever before, and this daughter of a Soviet hero was obviously terrified to do so. I was so shaken by her genuine fear that I could not restrain the tears flooding my own eyes.

There remained such a powerful longing among the Jews of Birobidzhan for the sound of the Yiddish word that not even terror could stifle it or uproot it. Somehow they managed to obtain official permission for a meeting at which the Yiddish writers, just returned from the prison camps, would read their poems. The large reading room in the Sholom Aleichem Library was filled to capacity. The representative of the Department of Culture and Education, speaking in Russian, was interrupted continuously by shouts of "Yiddish! Yiddish!" The audience was electrified by the readings, applauding wildly, demanding more, more. These simple men and women, casting off the oppressive years of fear, embraced the Yiddish writers as long-lost brothers who had come home.

An official invitation was delivered to me at my job in the clothing factory. The MGB wanted to see me. In order to allay my fears, the communication hastened to inform me that I was being called in only so they could return certain documents taken from me at the time of my arrest. I recalled that among the things taken when they searched my home were many poems still in manuscript.

When I was admitted to the office of the MGB, a major was listening to a radio broadcast about the most recent decisions of the Communist Party Central Committee, among which was a condemnation of the MGB for its illegal treatment of innocent people. The major turned off his radio and politely invited me to have a seat. He apologized for inconveniencing me and then handed me a small envelope containing a few personal photographs and some unimportant papers.

"And the manuscripts?" I asked.

"Concerning those you'll have to speak with your investigator. I'm new here. I had nothing to do with your case," he added with exaggerated affability. "Your investigator was transferred out to Kamchatka. He's working in the militia."

Thus I learned that my tormentor had been demoted and exiled to Kamchatka. At least I had lived long enough to enjoy a small measure of revenge on that repulsive, detestable flunky.

A tragic accident suddenly befell the Jews of Birobidzhan. Their only synagogue burned to the ground. Not that there had been a congregation as such around the synagogue. On Rosh Hashanah and Yom Kippur the synagogue was filled with Jews, including some young people, but on the Sabbath only a few older people showed up for services.

The fire had started in a workshop next door. Several adjacent buildings also were destroyed. Luckily the Torah scrolls in the synagogue were saved by several of the worshipers, who plunged into the burning building to rescue whatever they could. The sky over Birobidzhan was red with the flames consuming the last fortress of Jewishness that the older generation had been safeguarding at great sacrifice to themselves. Later they rented a little house somewhere and maintained an island of traditional Judaism in the desert that was left by the destruction of modern Jewish culture in the Jewish Autonomous Region.

In the Birobidzhan library, which once had housed thousands of Yiddish and Hebrew books plus a Judaica department in several European languages, only a few humiliated shelves of Yiddish books were now visible. All the books of the Soviet Yiddish authors—Bergelson, Markish,

---

Fefer, Kvitko, Der Nister—had been confiscated and burned. The Judaica material was rotting in a cellar. In fear of arrest (and possibly worse), Jews had destroyed their own Jewish libraries. Only a few brave Birobidzhan Jews managed to save a small number of books by burying them. One of these people proudly showed me a volume of Chaim Nachman Bialik's poems. The book was damp and moldy from years of hiding in a cellar.

Everything of a Jewish nature that had been accumulated in the Birobidzhan museum was thrown out. All the Jewish religious objects, gathered so painstakingly by the old Yiddish writer Boris Slutski, were destroyed.

Devoid of Jewish content also were the half-hour Yiddish radio broadcasts. What the listeners heard were only boring production reports from collective farms and industrial enterprises, reports of plans fulfilled, lists of Stakhanovite workers. Not one Yiddish word to warm the heart or lift the spirit; not a single mention of Jews in other parts of the world.

Is the Birobidzhan chapter really ended? Will the Soviet government no longer be able to lure Jews to Birobidzhan and then accuse them of nationalism? Birbodizhan was recently in the news once more—again there were calls to Jews to "come and build their Autonomous Region." The Moscow radio on several occasions has featured Jews who appealed for settlement in Birobidzhan. Nothing will ever come of this. The Jews in the Soviet Union know better.

Moscow–Warsaw–New York

At last. I am crossing the ocean on the Greek ship
New York. When one is already on the ocean, of what consequence is the name of the ship? But my future depends on
this ship. Somewhere below, people are dancing, enjoying
themselves. The sounds of the orchestra reach me on deck,
where I stand all alone in the night, between placid sky and
turbulent waves.

The ship's doctor, a Greek, confided in me today that
he had translated Rainer Maria Rilke's *Book of Hours* into
Greek. Apparently I am not the only one who is in love with
Rilke. Thousands regard him as the greatest poet of the
century.

I stand on deck staring at the waves. I want to forget
about myself, but I can't. My whole life unfurls here before
me like a scroll. My present mood corresponds exactly to
the words of another great poet whose work I love very
much, our own Israel Shtern, who wrote in his introduction
to the poem "Ostrolenka":

> Perhaps he must arise in riches
> Immersed and purified.
> Lonely he must keep his distance.
> So long as the wool remains unshorn
> We cannot begin to spin.
> And if everything is lost,
> Perhaps he'll yet find God.

Who knows what his sadness means?
He lies somewhere near a plain,
An alien, rejected plain,
And wrapped in darkness
As in an outspread robe, he keeps
All the parts the world has broken
Into tiny pieces—and he weeps.

I stand on deck. The ocean churns below me, demanding an answer to my lost years. As is normal, I want to remember only the bright moments of my life, but memory is now a wind that turns the pages of my life against my will. And now I'm at the end, looking backward, backward, at all my disappointed dreams.

On my way from Birobidzhan I stopped in Moscow for one day. Where should I go in Moscow, whom should I see there? Should I go to Gorky Street, where the walls in Peretz Markish's home still weep? Should I go to Lavrushinska, where the frames of all the windows on the big red building at Number 17 are mourning bands for Bergelson? And on Naroseyka Street? There the gentle Leib Kvitko no longer will greet me with a smile; his smile was drowned in blood somewhere in the dungeons of the Liubanka. I cannot even visit Ezra Finenberg, who was lucky enough to die a natural death.

In Moscow I see brand new neighborhoods, built since I left the city in 1944. But even the older parts of the city look strange to me, alien. I still am living in the barracks, my weary eyes still are fixed on Siberian snowfields where many Moscow citizens, along with me, shared the bitter fate of those execrable slave camps.

Yes, I did pay a visit in Moscow to one good friend from the camps. He had been released before me. When two ex-convicts meet in freedom, they feel like brothers. He has regained some of his strength and looks a little better than he did in the taiga. Now I am in his home. His wife and children are setting the table. This man, a Jew, is an engineer, but he cannot get his job back. His children are grown, they are working, they support the household. I cannot bear the sadness in my friend's blue eyes.

"Those who were there," he tells me, "will never again know peace of mind. I have nightmares in which my prison clothes are glued to my body and I cannot get them off."

I try to comfort him, although it takes a great effort on my part to overcome my own dejection. I keep praising him to his wife. I tell him he still looks youthful. My words have no effect. His eyes remain deep pools of sorrow. As we say goodbye at the train, we both sob.

I am standing on deck. The ocean continues its eternal roaring and rushing. On this ocean the skeptic Nathan Birenbaum became a believer. Why do I demand so much? Why can I not make peace with the thought that my people's limbs have been severed? Is that what has turned me, a believer, into a skeptic? But all my senses are so near to God. I feel His presence within me like a melody. I recognize His awesome beauty here in the middle of the ocean. When I left Him I turned away from myself, and now I cannot find myself again.

This irresistable protest grew even stronger within me when I stepped onto the soil of the country where the most creative part of my people was cut down so horribly. The bright moment of seeing the printed Yiddish word in Poland —a newspaper, a magazine, books, a Yiddish theater performance, after so many years away from all this—was darkened for me by the tragic loneliness of the small Jewish community in that country that once had held more than three million Jews. And what Jews they were! What a vibrant Jewish life was destroyed here!

In vain I searched in my native shtetl of Ostrów Mazowiecka for some trace of that Jewish way of life, with all its

color and variety. Ten thousand Jews lived in my town before the war. Now I found two. Two men. One was from
another town, here only by accident. The other had survived in the forest during the German occupation, but now
he was mentally unbalanced. His former home had been returned to him, so he moved about aimlessly within its walls
like a shadow. From time to time he went out to the place
where the old synagogue once stood and poked around
among the heaps of rubble as if he wanted to dig up everything that had been buried there forever.

My blood freezes as I look at the place where, at the
end of 1939, the Nazis shot more than six hundred Ostrów
Jews, among them my mother, Chaya Sara. All the Jews
were buried there in one mass grave. And on the barricaded
four-sided avenue with the lake in the middle, where I used
to walk in my youth and dream my magical dreams, the
Nazis dragged the Jews out of their synagogues on Yom
Kippur and forced them to wash the German army trucks.

How can the kind words and conciliatory acts of my
Polish friends ease my lacerated spirit? Still, what about the
Polish woman who had risked her own life to hide Jews
from death? There were good Christians too, certainly, but
very few, so few I cannot even make an accounting. But I
do demand an accounting from Him with whom I now stand
eye to eye between sky and water.

The ship glides and the ocean roars. Now we are ap-
proaching New York, home of the most populous Jewish
community in the world. Soon I will meet members of my
family whom I have not seen in many years but who never
left my mind's eye during the most difficult days in prison
and in the camps.

My father, of blessed memory, left our shtetl of Ostrów in 1919 to make a home for us in New York. A few
years later he died there. He had come looking for a home
for his lyrical holiness. A son-in-law of the Parisow rebbe, he

possessed that holiness in sufficient measure—more than he needed—in the old country. I, on the other hand, have come here with an abundance of the profane, searching for a little bit of holiness, for a tranquil Jewish life, which I yearn for so deeply and from which I estranged myself of my own free will. I search for it as if seeking vengeance on myself for the extinguished candles on my mother's Sabbath table.

Meanwhile I am still between sky and water, and the ocean roars its eternal complaint. In my mind I grope for Israel Shtern's wonderful lines:

And wrapped in darkness
As in an outspread robe, he keeps
All the parts the world has broken
Into tiny pieces—and he weeps.